"Chris Allaun's new book, "Upperworld", is a very interesting and
informative read. Consistent with his previous work, Chris focuses
on the myths, legends and spiritual teachings of an eclectic mix
of cultures from around the world, giving insights into their ways
of viewing the "higher" realms. Chris gives information on the
Shamanic world-view and the place of the Upperworld within it,
detailing techniques to access and explore its various realms.
Drawing on diverse sources, he not only describes the denizens
of the various realms of the gods, angels, stars, planets and
kabbalistic worlds, but gives practical information on how to make
contact and interact with them. There are rites of worship, magic,
devotion, astral projection and healing that not only give an insight
into the practical working of pagan, Shamanic experience, but
enable the reader to experience these themselves and take their
own journey along the Shamanic path. This is an accessible and
approachable work, both for the newcomer to the subject and the
more experienced practitioner alike; both will derive benefit from
reading this book."

-Nigel G. Pearson, author of *Treading the Mill: Workings of Traditional Witchcraft* and *The Devil's Plantation: East Anglian Lore, Witchcraft, and Folk-Magick*

"Ancient shamans didn't spend all their time journeying through the hazards of the underworld. They also took time to explore the heavens (or "Upperworld"), to learn the mysteries of creation, healing, and magick directly from the gods. It is refreshing, in this time when goetia is given so much focus, to see the author's exploration of the concepts and spiritual beings of the celestial realms. Just as important, his focus upon lore, legend, and mythology in developing a true understanding of and shamanic relationship with these beings is vital, and often missed in modern Western occult texts."

- Aaron Leitch, author of *Secrets of the Magical Grimoires: The Classical Texts of Magick Deciphered* and *The Essential Enochian Grimoire: An Introduction to Angelic Magick from Dr. John Dee to the Golden Dawn*

Upperworld: Shamanism and Magick of the Celestial Realms

Cover art/design Amanda Manesis www.amaradulcis.com

Other works by Chris Allaun

Underworld: Shamanism, Myth, and Magick vol I

Deeprer Into the Underworld: Death, Ancestors, and Magical Rites

Contents

Illustrations 5

Introduction 7

1   Magick of the Heavens 10

2   Creation 37

3   The Heavens 59

4   The Gods 85

5   Angels 113

6   Higher Beings 143

7   Stars 162

8   Planets 187

9   Universal and Spiritual Energies 223

    Conclusion 245

    Bibliography 247

    Index 251

Upperworld Illustrations

P. 10 Upperworld by Amanda Manesis

P. 37 Creation by Amanda Manesis

P. 59 Flowers of the Tree of Life by Amanda Manesis

P. 72 Kabbalistic Tree of Life by Amanda Manesis

P. 85 Offerings to the Gods by Jeff Cullen

P. 113 Raphael by Joseph Ahn

P. 117 Raphael, Michael, Gabriel, Ariel by Joseph Ahn

P. 132 Melek Taus by Joseph Ahn

P. 143 Thunder Beings by Larry Phillips

P. 162 Gazing at the Stars by Jeff Cullen

P. 187 Magick of the Moon by Larry Phillips

P. 192 Coyote Steals Tobacco by Larry Phillips

P. 223 The Universe by Larry Phillips

Introduction

Prometheus (Greco-Roman)

Prometheus watched over mankind. In those days, humans had no tools, no weapons, and no fire. They could not cook their food or make tools for planting or harvesting. They could not defend themselves from wild beasts save for the crude weapons they made with sticks and rocks. Day after day, Prometheus watched as men barely survived and had much suffering. Food was scarce and enemies were everywhere. It saddened Prometheus to watch his beloved humans to work so hard for survival.

In the heavens, the gods had many wondrous things. They had mighty weapons and fast chariots. They had beautiful ornaments and magnificent jewelry. They had grand palaces and lovely instruments. All of these things were made from the magick of fire. Prometheus would look around himself and see all the wonders of the gods and at the same time see the cold dark sufferings of his beloved humans. He knew what he had to do! He must sacrifice this magick to the men and women on earth. From the sun's chariot, he lit a magical torch and brought it down from heaven and gave it to the earth and to mankind. He taught them how to use this wonderful technology. With this magick, humans cooked their food and warmed their homes, but the hearts of men found a weapon with this power. They fashioned weapons to destroy their enemies. They burned forests to raise livestock. They would eventually create bombs that had the potential to destroy the earth and all humans with it.

Zeus saw that he had been tricked and that Prometheus had given humans fire. They were not ready for such magick, such power. For his treachery, Zeus bound Prometheus to the side of a mountain. Every day a great eagle would eat out this liver and every night it would grow back so that Prometheus could endure this horrid torture for the rest of eternity. For Prometheus, he was giving his beloved humans a godly gift, but to Zeus, he had given them their own damnation.

Stealing Fire From Heaven

Stealing magical things from heaven has always been one of my favorite parts of mythology. There are some gods, angels, and higher beings who wish to see humanity and the world flourish. There are many things that we have that is said to have come from the gods such as fire, wine, chocolate, technology, magick, and healing. But there are many Upperworld beings that do not trust mankind and will guard their treasures with their lives. In the case of Prometheus, he wanted humans to have the same advantages that the gods did. But because he cared for them so much he could not see that some men would use fire to destroy rather than build. This is ironic because the name Prometheus means *forethought*.

Shamans, witches, and magicians have obtained a lot of magical and spiritual information from the Upperworld. One of the reasons a magician would work with angelic beings is because they have wisdom and magick about the universe and the stars. From a scientific point of view, another way to explain angels is to think of them as specific energies and motion of the universe. Shamans will often journey to the Upperworld so that may learn healing techniques from the gods themselves. One of my patron gods is Asclepius, the Greco-Roman God of healing. He can be seen as the rising sun that dispels the darkness (disease/ death). I have journeyed many times to his healing temple in the Upperworld. The magick of the seven planets has much wisdom and power to offer. Each planet and its intelligence can teach you the art of magick, science, love, war, sacrifice, success, and death. This is the fire from the gods.

The Upperworld is one of the most talked about subjects in magick. However when one begins to research this subject there are countless books of Hermetic and Kabbalistic magick with its complicated formulas, chants, and correspondences. This became popular with the Golden Dawn back in the latter 1800's. The formula for this type of magick come with many warnings of "don't do it wrong!" or "don't say the wrong words or else!" In my years of magical experience I have found that most of these warnings are silly and were designed for the former Christian to feel "safe" performing magick. Don't get me wrong, there are many dangerous things in magick but to those of us who know the difference between safety and fear, we can distill the teachings of the celestial realms to a more tangible workable system. There are also many books on astrology that are wonderful and my goal is not to regurgitate something already written, but to teach a new way of looking at the magick of the stars and planets.

My goal with this book is to teach Upperworld magick in a way that shamans, witches, and ceremonial magicians can discover new techniques or become inspired to improve on some of their favorites. I am presenting to you how I approach the Upperworld with my blend of shamanism, kabbalistic magick, and witchcraft with some good old fashioned storytelling. I invite you to reach out with your heart, spirit, and soul to the stars and the world above and meet the gods. They have been waiting for you.

1
Magick
of the
Heavens

The sky is a place of inspiration and awe. From the brilliance and warmth of the sun to the mysterious glow of stars deep in space. The energies from the world above touch our spirit in deep and profound ways. The heavens are a place of wonder and magick. The rising and setting of the sun gives us illumination and the waxing and waning of the moon pore out energies that affect our magick. Every day we are affected by celestial phenomenon, such as the movement of the planets and the constellations, that travel over us by night. We are connected to the dance of the cosmos. The energies of the stars and planets are sent to us from the depths of space and, at times, affect our thoughts and emotions. They inspire us to know what is in the above world.

When ancient shamans journeyed above, they saw that this was the place of the gods, angels, and many other spirits that aide in the evolution of the Universe. The energies that keep the cosmos in motion were seen as great beings of power and motion to early shamans. These great powers could be communicated with in order to better the tribe. These celestial beings could speak of future events as well as teach humanity the secrets of the creation. In modern times, we walk a shamanic path not only to better our community, but to also better ourselves. We journey to the Upperworld so that we may meet our gods, speak with angels, understand the planets, and summon higher beings in order to heal ourselves and our earth. We journey to the Upperworld so that we may seek wisdom and spiritually evolve.

The first spiritual question that people ask themselves, or their deity, is "Why am I here? And where did I come from?" When we are children, we are told things like "God has a plan" or "No one is to know God's will". These things offer little comfort to those of us who know that we are meant for something more. We know that our path is going to filled with adventure and magick. However, we are not quite sure how that will manifest. But, there is a deep "knowing" in our bellies. While growing up, we are interested in the fantasy, magick, and adventure. We may or may not mingle with society easily. Even when we enter the higher grades of school we know we are meant for something bigger that is presented to us by our parents and teachers but we cannot explain it. We may try, but we are laughed at or are told that we are just day dreamers and that we need to do something more practical. If you have tried to join the rest of society by doing something more practical then you may have succeeded. Magickal people tend to succeed in anything they put their minds too. Some say it is the magick within us trying to get out. I tend to believe that it is because we are more determined to succeed than most people. Perhaps this is the nature of magick. Eventually, we seek our own paths. If you were anything like me, then you started your journey with the basic books on magick and "alternative" spirituality and branched on from there. The rest of it is a crazy, wonderful journey to where we are now and beyond. But first we ask, "Why am I here? Where did I come from?"

Three Worlds

In the shamanic worldview, there are three major worlds. There is the Upperworld, Middleworld, and the Underworld. These three worlds are sometimes symbolized by a World Tree. The branches and leaves contain the Upperworld, the trunk is the Middleworld, and the roots are the Underworld. In myths of the Nordic people, the world tree, named Yggdrasil, is very real to them and is not merely a symbol. If we take a closer look at the energetic and physical properties of the tree, such as an ash or oak, we can easily see how some shamans saw the Universe as a great tree.

Let us start with the base of the tree trunk or the Middleworld.

The tree trunk is the first thing we are able to touch when we approach a mighty tree. It seems hard and dense. The middle world is very dense and is the only world that is physical. It is also the only part of the tree that is "round". Our world is cyclical in nature. It has seasons and moon cycles that never end. The roots below go deep within the earth in search for water. Our ancestors are buried in the ground and the fertilization of the dead give the tree life. The waters are a mystery into healing and magick. There are also undesirable things that live in the ground such as insects, worms, and snakes. These things add to the mythology of the World Tree. The branches above go high into the skies. The worlds of the gods. The green leaves gather the sunlight and the cosmic energies of the planets and galaxies for the nutrients for the Mighty Tree. The Upperworld gathers fire. The Underworld gathers water. The Middleworld puts them all together in balance for life.

Middleworld

The world we live in, the physical world and more, is the Middleworld. This is the place of the four elements, the cycles of life, death, and rebirth, and the many life forms that make up our natural world. The Middleworld has two main parts: the physical and the astral, sometimes called the Otherworld. They physical world contains everything that we can touch, smell, see, taste, and hear with our physical five senses. It is the word of humans, animals, plant life, stones, waters, and insects. All of these things have a sacred and divine purpose. The astral side of the Middleworld contains the Faery folk, elves, nature spirits, spirits of place, and many more spirits.

These beings of the Middleworld are often seen on the magical nights where astrological forces are strong for such things such as full moons, pagan festival days, and the solstices and equinoxes. There are many stories of travelers meeting faeries or elves during these holy nights. In Shamanic cosmologies, the Midworld is sometimes portrayed as the trunk of a great cosmic tree.

Underworld

The Underworld is the place of the ancestors, chthonic deities, healing, demons, and sometimes monsters. It was observed that upon death, the body dissolved back into the earth so it was concluded that the spirit must also return to the earth to a place of rest and rejuvenation. There are also parts of the Underworld that are a prison for beings that are too chaotic for the Middle or Upper worlds. These chthonic entities roamed the Midworld when chaos reigned. When the energies of the Universe evolved to be more "orderly", the new gods of justice and order imprisoned the old gods of chaos in the Underworld so they would not cause destruction upon the Universe. Demons are also in the Underworld. In Judeo-Christian cosmology, demons are the angels that were banished from heaven after the Great War. In my experience and research, I have not found this to be so. Demons were created for a greater purpose just as other entities are. In Shamanic cosmologies, the Underworld is portrayed as the roots of a great cosmic tree.

Upperworld

The Upperworld is the place of gods and goddesses, angels, planets, galaxies, stars, and other celestial energies. This is the place of creation. Some say the Upperworld is the place of the divine, but I believe that all worlds are divine. The gods resonate on a "higher" vibration than the Middle or Underworld so they naturally belong to the place of the stars. The cosmic universe is vast and mysterious and so, too, are the gods. It is believed that it was the divine that created the Universe and the stars, so naturally the stars would be their home.

The Upperworld is thought to be the place of spiritual evolution, healing helpers, holy medicine people, and guardian angels. For many, this is the place they wish to be upon death; next to god. In shamanic cosmology the Upperworld is associated with the branches of the great cosmic tree.

Why Journey To The Upperworld?

Journeying to the Upperworld is one of the most fulfilling experiences you may have while in the astral plane. It has been spoken about in many different religions. Jesus ascended to heaven after he arose from the dead. Native American Shamans have traveled to the sky to meet with the Thunder Beings, and in Kabbalistic mysticism, magicians travel the spheres of the tree of life to be one with God. To be in the Upperworld is to be closer to the gods, angels, and higher beings. It is a place of divine inspiration, poetry, and healing. Shamans, magicians, and witches have traveled to this wonderful place to move beyond the limitations of the physical plane and find to connect with the gods.

One of the more common reasons modern shamans travel to the Upperworld is to seek council with the gods. Gods and goddesses are immortal and have magnificent powers. They also transcend time and space and often look over humanity as well as all life on earth. They can give us guidance on our spiritual path and help us commune with them in a deeper way. In neo-paganism, the gods are considered to be the most powerful of beings and can help you obtain things you may need in life as well as wisdom and spiritual evolution. Another reason is that we can create relationship with entities such as angels, ascended masters, healers, ascended ancestors, and other higher beings. These entities understand and control the energies of the Uppperworld and of the universe. They are older than time itself and can help you understand the function of the universe as well as deep and profound wisdom. They do not have as much power as the gods, but each of these spirits has a divine purpose that may be able to help us on our chosen path.

By traveling to the Upperworld we can learn the interconnection of all things, sometimes referred to as the "cosmic web". With this, we can learn more about our own Fate/ Destiny and the spiritual path that we have have chosen. Perhaps we have chosen this path in a former life or in between lives. The Upperworld can help us understand our divine purpose and why we are here on earth. We can work with spirits that can give us direction and guide us to living a more fulfilling spiritual life.

There are also many places in the Upperworld that we can visit that humans do not know about. There are places in the deep universe that are uncharted by astronomers that are too distant for us to find. By using our shamanic powers, we can travel to remote places in the space and distant galaxies at the speed of thought. There are constellations and star portals that are home to many life forms, both physical and spiritual.

By traveling to the Upperworld we can discover things about the universe and ourselves that we would never be able to do otherwise. The universe is ever expanding out into the deep reaches of space. Energies and other dimensions are evolving at a faster and faster rate. By learning about the Upperworld we can heal ourselves, our community, and help humanity in its spiritual evolution.

The Higher Self

The primary tool of the shaman is our mind. I think of our minds as like a computer monitor telling us what is happening to us in the other worlds when we are journeying. Yes, we are actually there in the energy/ spirit worlds but we are perceiving things through our physical brains. This is one of the reasons that we are able to journey to the Upperworld, yet hear what is going on around us in the physical world. This is also one of the reasons that the shamanic drum beat can keep us in trance while we journey.

This poses the question, are we making it all up and we are just fooling ourselves? Say, for argument's sake, that we are just visualizing things in our minds and nothing more. There is still a value to this type of work. I have found that shamanistic magick and healing to be very authentic, but for those people who think it is simply an exercise in psychology, then great! You will find much healing and value with this type of work. Let's take a moment to look at how the shamanistic universe is related to the aspect of the mind and consciousness. Our everyday thinking, waking mind is related to the Midworld. This is our daily perceptions and five senses of sight, smell, taste, touch, and hearing. This is also our inner monologue and our hopes, dreams, fears, prejudices, and desires. The Underworld is related to our subconscious and our shadow self. This is the part of our consciousness that is more "hidden" from us; including, our repressed fears, sorrow, and hidden desires. There are many times we have desires that we are not even aware of. This is why when we travel to the Underworld we are sometimes encountered by demons and monsters. These are representations of our repressed fears and memories we do not wish to confront in our everyday waking consciousness.

The Upperworld is related to our higher consciousness or our higher selves. Some spiritual people say that our higher self is a spark of the divine or *Buddha consciousness*. Personally, I believe that the higher self is your *true* self. The self that remains constant life after life. The self that is connected to the Universal matrix of evolution and higher being. I believe that the higher self is aware of your everyday comings and goings and its purpose is to help you spiritually evolve without interfering in your own natural process of growth. The higher self is also connected to the *collective consciousness* that connects everyone in your community, your country, and the world. I believe that is what people are referring to when they say that we have a guardian angel or the Kabbalistic Holy Guardian Angel. It's you. Just the higher spiritual aspect of you.

So, if we are just imagining everything , then we have a wonderful tool to have conversations with our higher self. This is an amazing opportunity to discover your true purpose in life and understand your Divine Will. Your Divine Will is the spiritual purpose that you incarnated on earth in this life and subsequent lives. Your daily or everyday will is different from this. Your daily will tells you what you want for lunch, what kind of car you would like, and where you want to go to relax. Your Divine Will is a calling that tells you how to help people and yourself grow and heal spiritually. Ideally, the job you have will be congruent with your Divine Will. Perhaps you are a teacher, a spiritual leader, a healer, a shaman, or warrior. Perhaps it is your Divine Will to be a lawyer to help defend the innocent or punish the guilty. The only person who can tell you what your Divine Will is is you. By journeying to speak with your higher self you are on your way to discovering what your Divine Will is truly.

Upperworld Entrances

Finding an entrance to the Upperworld can be very easy. When we look at the great shamanic tree it is easy to see that the branches of the tree reach high into the heavens. Shamans can use any tree if they like. I prefer a tree that goes way up into the sky. I have often used red wood trees because of their enormous size. You can also use other things as well. If you are inclined towards the Egyptian pantheon you can use the pyramids. As I discussed in my previous book *Underworld: Shamanism, Myth, and Magick*, the pyramids were designed as a portal to the otherworlds after the pharaoh's death. You can use the point of a pyramid as a launching pad into the Upperworld. You can use standing stones the same way as you would use the tree branches. For modern, shamans you can use tall buildings and skyscrapers. Being from Chicago, we have some of the largest buildings in the world. Willis Tower, in downtown Chicago, stretches way into the clouds, especially when the clouds are low on a rainy day.

Another way you can journey into the Upperworld is through the broom or a shamanic staff. In order to do this, you sit astride the broom grasping the handle, the brush part behind you. Then, while holding the broom, place the broom handle on your forehead. If you are using a shamanic staff, simply place your forehead upon the staff while holding it upright. Take a breath and accumulate the power into your head. On the exhale, quickly and forcefully project your consciousness (astral body) out through your third eye, into the broom/ staff, and out of the top of the handle and into the Upperworld.

You may also simply gaze at the stars at night. You can place yourself in a light trance and project yourself into the Upperworld. When I was in college, I lived in a small town north of Dallas, Texas called Denton. One night, I had a dream that a Native American woman was teaching me how to astral project. There was a large tree in the back of my apartment building that we sat under. She explained to me, that to astral project, we must sit under the tree and gaze at the stars through the tree branches. Once you have found a star that calls to you as a guide, you must visualize yourself rising up through the tree branches into the stars all the while staring at your guiding star. I did as I was instructed and I astral projected for the first time into the heavens.

The Upperworld has its own rules as does the Underworld. It is sometimes more abstract than the Underworld or Midworlds. The Midworld is the closest to the physical plane and it also in the "middle" of the worlds, as its name suggests, so it feels the most balanced to humans. The Underworld can feel heavy and also feels like you are in a dream. Things are often obscured or hidden in the Underworld. There are many illusions and the energy you have in your mind, heart, and spirit is projected outward. This is why we see demonic beings as well as images from our hopes and fears. The Upperworld is different. If the Underworld feels like a dream, then the Upperworld can feel like a fever dream. This is a place of higher beings, angels, gods, ascended ancestors and healers and planetary spirits. Their concern is with the order of the universe and the evolution of all species, including humans. The Upperworld is a place of light and power. But it can also have its dark places. Black holes, supernovas, and the darkest reaches of space may not be the most safe for us to travel to, yet they are curious places. You would not be reading this book if you were not curious about strange, wonderful, and dangerous places. We travel to the Upperworld for knowledge, power, magick, and wisdom.

Mythology of the Upperworld

Myths are the stories that once came from the shaman. The shaman or medicine person travels to the three worlds and finds wisdom, power, and healing and brings it back to the tribe. The shaman has the ability to travel to strange universes and dimensions to speak with the spirits who dwell there. In shamanistic psychology, the three worlds are linked to our levels of consciousness. The Midworld is linked to our everyday consciousness, or waking mind. The Underworld is linked to our subconsciousness , or our shadow self. And the Upperworld is linked to our super our higher consciousness, or our spiritual self. Our higher self speaks to us in symbols, archetypes and dreams. Everything in our universe is made up of energy. From gamma rays to radio waves to the earth itself; the universe is energy. The subtle energies of the Upperworld, not only are difficult to see with our physical eyes, but are difficult to comprehend with our minds as well.

The gods, angels, planetary spirits, and so forth are all energy. Our minds take these abstract energies and tries to make sense of it the best it can. This is why the gods always look like the people of that culture. The Nordic gods appear to be prepared for harsh snows and storms, the Greek gods are barely dressed in togas, and the Egyptian gods are adorned with headdresses of gold. Our mind dresses the gods and spirits in a form that is appealing to each one of us. This is why it is perfectly acceptable to modernize gods and goddess to wear Prada dresses and Armani suits. The gods and spirits choose to appear as we do so that we are more comfortable with them and can communicate with each other easier. In some myths, when the gods reveal their true form the power is so strong that the onlooker is vaporized or burned to death. This is one of the reasons the gods appear to us in human form.

Myths are universal. In my book *Underworld: Shamanism, Myth, and*

Magick, I showed how myths of the Underworld from around the world were similar because the human experience of death and the afterlife are similar. This is because all humans have the same desires, wants, needs, and fears. Our landscapes and environments might be different but our experiences are the same. We all need to eat, find shelter, love, and die. In the book *The Power of Myth,* Joseph Campbell says, "The ancient myths were designed to harmonize the mind and the body. The mind can ramble off in strange ways and want things the body does not want. The myths and rites were a means of putting the mind in accord with the body and the way of life in accord with the way that nature dictates." In his book, *Pathways To Bliss,* he says, "Mythological images are the images by which the consciousness is put in touch with the unconscious."

When we view myths from the point of view of journeying to the Upperworld and working with higher spiritual powers, they take on a more transformative meaning than simply stories of our everyday life. They teach us how to work with the gods in a more personal way. Myths will tell us what the gods like and do not like. They show us how some failed to appease the gods while others became a favorite of the gods. According to *Aradia: Gospel of the Witches* by Charles Leland, Diana, the goddess of the moon, granted one of her followers a husband for being so devoted to her. They will also give cautionary tales. We all know the story of how Icarus used wings bound with wax to fly into the skies and how, as he flew too close to the sun, the wings began to melt and he came tumbling down to his death.

Often, when we say something is a myth, we say it is not true or a fictionalized story. Myths were never meant to be dogma as in the Christian Bible, but are meant to teach Universal energies, ethics of a certain people or culture, and the experiences of humans and animals upon the earth. Myths are "living" stories. The Universal laws do not change so; therefore, the myths do not change. This is one of the reasons why the myths of ages past are still relevant today. Yes, it is true that people evolve and grow, but we still have the same behaviors and psychological make up as we did thousands of years ago. We are still falling in love and we are still going to war over land, power, and religion. Myths are relevant to the past as well as the present *and* future.

But what role does the shaman play with myths when it pertains to the Upperworld? How can we as shamans, magicians, and witches, take these stories and powers and heal community as well as ourselves? I think, first, we start with the hero's journey. The hero, in myth, is always an ordinary person with no special abilities or powers who hears the call of the spirits or gods. I personally call this the "call of the wild". This is when you feel a call to do, or become, more than you are. This may mean becoming an artist, a doctor, a priestess, or healer. The call is so strong that sometimes you can become obsessed by it. What this means is that you can sometimes become consumed with the desire to become more. This may manifest as taking classes or moving to a place that is more "suited" for your chosen profession such as an actor moving to New York. The hero's journey is never easy. To become greater you must face greater things. You must confront life circumstances that challenge your experiences and way of thinking. This can be very difficult. It is far easier to stay in the safety of the village then it is to journey into the deep dark forest with its wolves and monsters. Yet, at the end of the adventure is the magical grail, or your spiritual calling.

When we take this idea and apply it to the Upperworld, we are working with the gods and higher spirits that work with the fabric of the Universe as well as our personal destiny. The myths will prepare you for the celestial spirits above. However, they will not tell you what is going to happen in the Upperworld, they will give you clues on the energies and temperaments of each spirit you encounter. For example, when you meet the Greek sun god, Apollo, he will not endure the arrogance of men. There is a story of how a man could play the Lyre so beautifully he often boasted that he could even out play Apollo, the god of music and healing. Hearing the man's arrogance, Apollo challenged him to a contest. First the man played with such grace and magic that all were hypnotized by his talent. But then when Apollo played the lyre he played the very music of the Universe and the magick of the cosmos. None could dispute the winner. For the poor man's arrogance, Apollo had him skinned alive. This is an extreme case, but it shows without a doubt what Apollo will put up with.

As we journey into the heavens, keep in mind the myths. They are symbols and stories yet they are true. True in the effect that our minds have filtered these energies into stories that begin to help us comprehend a Universe that is so much greater than ourselves. The myths are ancient, but they are living. Living because the Universe is living. So, go forth and begin creating your own myths.

Navigating The Upperworld

Navigating the Upperworld can be both very simple and complex at the same time. If we use the image of the shamanic world tree, we know that if we use the great branches they will lead up us to the worlds and Universes above. The Upperworld is as big as it is beautiful. There are many places you will want to visit and I am not sure if any shaman or magician has ever discovered all the wonderful and mysterious places there are in this wonderful creation that we sometimes call the *Multiverse*. The Upperworld is mirrored by the cosmos and we know from astronomy and astrophysics that our Universe is ever expanding, becoming larger and larger by the second. There are so many possibilities of discovery and so many opportunities for spiritual evolution and power.

Many students of shamanism run into some stumbling blocks when they are first journeying to the worlds above. When I first started journeying to the Upperworld, I would find myself in the clouds and no further. There are many spirits in the skies of our world such as the Native American Thunder People and many sky gods and goddesses from around the world. Thor, Zeus, Ra, and Father Sky are only a small few. But there is so much more. We must keep going into the depths of the Upperworlds. If you become blocked at going any further, an easy trick is to visualize the branches of the World Tree extending into deep space and even to other galaxies and dimensions.

It is important to work closely with your Upperworld guide and your totem. Learn from them. Allow them to help you map your way across the Universe. Mapping the Upperworld is not something we do literally. The Otherworlds are not like the physical plane so we cannot simply draw a directional map. The Three Shamanic Worlds are made of energy and we must remember that the way to map spiritual energy is through thought, memory, visualization, will, and desire. When we discover a new world or dimension, we have to remember what it looked like. It is also important to remember any smells, feelings, and sensations we associate with this place. Make sure you journal your experience when returning from an Upperworld journey. When we want to return, we must visualize where we want to go and have a strong Will to get there. Remember, as shamans, magicians, and witches we travel much faster than the speed of light. We travel at the speed of thought.

There are many things that can also help us along the way. We can use constellations and star portals as "road posts" to help us along the way. I am from Texas originally and there is the on going joke that we do not give directions by street names or numbers. Because we lived in the country we would say, "It's the second street on your left across from the red barn. Then turn left at the big oak tree. You know it's us because of the white pickup truck in the driveway." Navigating the Upperworld can be the same way. In the book *Peter Pan,* J.M. Barrie says, "Second star to the right and straight on 'till morning."

When we are traveling in the Upperworld you may discover:

1. The home of the gods

2. Angels and Ascended beings

3. Star portals and beings from other parts of the Galaxy, the Universe, and the Multiverse.

4. Places of Power and Knowledge

5. Planetary beings and intelligences

6. Powers of the constellations and Zodiac

7. Places of healing

The Egyptians believed that the physical world is a mirror image of the Upperworld. Not only did the gods make humans in their image, but so too did they make the world of humans in the image of the world of the gods. In his book *Land of the Fallen Star Gods: The Celestial Origins of Ancient Egypt,* J.S. Gordon says, "The allegorical importance of the Nile cannot be overly stressed because of its many metaphysical and cosmological associations with both the Milky Way and the constellation Draco, the dragon, or "The Flying Serpent". With this in mind, we can say parts of the earth are a reflection of the worlds above. The Upperworld in Europe will have mountains, the Upperworld over the desert will have vast spaces of canyons and valleys, while the Upperworld of the American Plains will be home to celestial plains. It is also safe to say that parts of the Upperworld will have large cities with tall buildings and the hustle and bustle of a large population.

Astral Projection and Shamanic Journeying

It is important that we learn how to journey out of our bodies, or astrally travel into the Upperworld. There is really no difference in journeying and astral travel. They both are more or less the same thing. *Journeying* is used in the earth-based shamanic communities and *astral projection* commonly used in new-age and magical communities. Terminology is not important here, but the use and development of the skill is.

When we leave our bodies to travel into the other worlds we do not need to be worried about our physical bodies. No evil spirit will come and try to possess our bodies or cause us harm. Our naturally strong auras and energy bodies will protect us from any spirit intrusion. Also, we will have complete awareness of our physical bodies and five senses. This is helpful because we can listen to a drum beat or a rattle to help keep us in a trance state. We can also speak with others if they ask us questions about our journey. When you are first learning to journey, I would suggest that you keep the talking to a bare minimum so that you can focus on the astral projection and the experience of the journey. You do not want to miss something because you were not paying attention.

Below are a few basic techniques to get you started. As you strengthen your astral projection skills, feel free to modify the techniques for yourself to fit your skill level. If you already have an astral projection technique you prefer, then please use that one instead.

Astral Exercise #1

1. It may be helpful to play a shamanic drumming recording. If you have someone to drum for you all the better. The drumming should be very light, but audible enough to hear comfortably. If you are using a drum or having someone drum for you, have them beat at a moderately quick pace. If for some reason you cannot get a recording of shamanic drumming, don't worry. It is not necessary to have a shamanic drum beat to astral project.

2. Sit or lie in a comfortable position. Make sure your back is as straight as possible.

3. Close your eyes and take a few deep breaths.

4. Relax your body as best you can. Begin with your feet. Tell them to relax and release all tension. Then move up to your calves. Tell them to relax and release all tension. Go up to the thigh, glutes, back, belly, chest, shoulders, arms, hands, neck, and head in turn, telling them all to relax and release all stress and tension.

5. Imagine yourself getting up and walking around. Remember, this is done entirely with your imagination. Try not to move your physical body at all.

6. Walk around the room you are in and look at the furniture, walls, shelves. Look at yourself. See yourself lying (or sitting) down.

7. When you are ready, see yourself walk over to your physical body and sit or lie back into yourself. When you are close to your body this will most often happen automatically.

Astral Exercise #2

1. Play your shamanic drumming recording if you have one as per

the previous exercise.

2. Sit or lie in a comfortable position. Make sure your back is as straight as possible.

3. Close your eyes and take a few deep breaths.

4. Relax your body as best you can. Begin with your feet. Tell them to relax and release all tension. Then move up to your calves. Tell them to relax and release all tension. Go up to the thigh, glutes, back, belly, chest, shoulders, arms, hands, neck, and head in turn, telling them all to relax and release all stress and tension.

5. Imagine yourself getting up and walking around. Remember, this is done entirely with your imagination. Try not to move your physical body at all.

6. At this point, see a door or gateway in front of you. Know that the door leads to the World Tree.

7. Step through the door and on the other side see the World Tree. The Word Tree is the largest tree you have ever seen. Its trunk extends out further than the eye can see going both left and right. The branches go up into the heavens and you cannot see the top of the tree. You can see that the roots go deep into the Earth.

8. This is the Center of the Middleworld, and it is your starting point. Until you are very proficient with traveling, you may want to start here.

9. Look above the mighty trunk and you will see the massive branches of World Tree. These branches go above into the clouds and deep into space and the cosmos. Each branch will lead you to a different part of the Upperworld. You can climb the tree branches or you can simply fly up.

10. Make sure you have your totem with you. Have a clear intention of where you want to explore in the Upperworld. If you intention is simply to explore the world above, state that intention to the spirits.

11. Finally, when you arrive at the Upperworld, take note of the first thing you see? Explore the immediate environments carefully. When you are ready, go back the way you came and back down the branches of the World Tree, then back to the Trunk of the Tree and into the Middle World.

12. After awakening from your journey, record your experience in your magickal journal and ground yourself back to the physical plane. You may do this by eating something light, drinking water, and/or doing "everyday" things around your home.

Astral Exercise #3

1. Play your shamanic drumming recording if you have one as per the previous exercises.

2. Sit or lie in a comfortable position. Make sure your back is as straight as possible.

3. Close your eyes and take a few deep breaths.

4. Relax your body as best you can. Begin with your feet. Tell them to relax and release all tension. Then move up to your calves. Tell them to relax and release all tension. Go up to the thigh, glutes, back, belly, chest, shoulders, arms, hands, neck, and head in turn, telling them all to relax and release all stress and tension.

5. Visualize a spiral of light, beginning at your feet, spiraling around you, going clockwise; it surrounds your entire body. The only

thing you are able to see is the spiral of light. Know that this magickal spiral of light is transporting you to the World Tree.

6. This is the Center of the Middle World, your starting point. Until you are very proficient with traveling, you always want to start here.

7. Look above the mighty trunk and you will see the massive branches of World Tree. These branches go above into the clouds and deep into space and the cosmos. Each branch will lead you to a different part of the Upperworld. You can climb the tree branches or you can simply fly up.

8. Make sure you have your totem with you. Have a clear intention of where you want to explore in the Upperworld. If you intention is simply to explore the world above, state that intention to the spirits.

9. Finally, when you arrive at the Upperworld, take note of the first thing you see? Explore the immediate environments carefully. When you are ready, go back the way you came and back down the branches of the World Tree, then back to the Trunk of the Tree and into the Middle World.

10. After awakening from your journey, record your experience in your magickal journal and ground yourself back to the physical plane. You may do this by eating something light, drinking water, and/or doing "everyday" things around your home.

Shamanic Totem

Our totem is our animalistic aspect of our soul. It is us if we were to be transformed into an animal. It is us, yet it is also separate from us. When we call upon our totem we can see it outside of us and it appears to have a distinct personality from us. In my experience, I have found that our totem is an aspect of our higher self that is connect to the three worlds. It has the ability to find spirits and lost soul shards as well as see into the energy fields and minds of the ancestors, spirits, angels, and gods. Just as a wild animal or guard dog has keen senses such as hearing, smell, and sight, so to does our totem. Our totem animal has the additional senses of the spirit world. My totem has gotten me out of many dangerous situations before they even started.

I have found that a person's totem is related to genetics as well as geographic location. For example, I am part Cherokee and my totem is the mountain lion; an animal that is indigenous to the Americas. If you look at my facial structure and personality, they you will notice many feline traits. The totem is you, not who you wish to be. If you disdain running then odds are you are not a jaguar or if you do not like trees then you are probably not a monkey. I have found it rare that someone's totem is a bird, fish, or bug. Although, I have seen it. Never say never, but it is extremely rare. One of my friend's mother is an owl. When you see her you can't NOT see Owl. It is her in every aspect.

Your totem will have many abilities. It will be able to sniff out danger and negative energies. There will be many times that how the spirits present themselves is not who they really are or really appear. Your totem will know this. Your totem will also know when you are in great danger. If he or she pulls you away from a gate or door, listen. It could be dangerous or perhaps you are not ready to deal with whatever is behind that door. Your totem will speak to you both on a soul level and within your mind. If you have a feeling your totem is telling you something, then you are probably right. Over time, you will learn to speak with your totem on a very deep spiritual level.

In the exercise below, I will give you a technique to find your totem.

When you are looking for your totem, you should see it on your journey a couple of times. Other animals may come up to you, but those may be animal helper spirits who wish to help you upon your path. Helpers are not you. Your totem is you. If you see animal helpers on your journey, mentally take note of them for a later date and continue on your journey to find your totem. When you find your totem it should feel like a homecoming. Like you knew it all along what your totem would be. When I take my students on this journey to find their totem, once they find it they usually say something like, "Oh my god! Of course it is! How could I not have known?"

Finding Your Totem Animal

For this exercise, you will travel to the Middle World in order to find your animal totem.

1. Choose one of the astral exercises from above and travel to the World Tree.

2. Once there, make the following statement: "I wish to find my animal totem"

3. Begin walking in whichever direction feels appropriate to you. Keep the goal of finding your totem in mind and try to intuit the direction you should go. The landscape will vary from person to person. You may find yourself traveling into a forest, mountains, valleys, or grass plains. Trust your instincts. For the time being, do not worry if you are "making it up." Visualize your surroundings to the best of your abilities.

4. Keep an eye out for any animals you see. You may see several. Some traditions say that you may see other animals, but you will see your totem animal four times as your walk along your path.

This is a good approach to take.

5. If you do not see any animals at first, keep walking. You should eventually begin to see more and more animals.

6. Once you see your totem four times along your path, walk up to it. Ask it, "Are you my totem?"

7. If the animal seems distant, unfamiliar, or unwilling to speak with you, then this may not be your totem. If it is not your totem, keep searching.

8. If the animal is your totem then it will feel like a long lost friend or relative. Your totem may even feel like a part of you. This is because in reality, your totem IS a part of you.

9. Ask your totem its name and record it in your magickal diary or journal upon returning to your physical body.

Once you are fully conscious, visualize your totem in front of you. You may choose to dance with it or simply imagine your animal totem combining with your aura. To combine the totem with your aura, visualize your animal in front of you. See him/her walking toward you and energetically combining itself with your aura. Know that you can call upon your totem at any time in any world! I recommend getting an animal fetish - a little statue of clay or stone that represents your animal. If you have the fur, teeth, or a claw of the animal then all the better. You can place these things in a medicine bag or simply place it on your altar.

Your Upperworld Guide

Your Upperworld guide is a very important ally you should have when you are journeying to the heavens. I have found that the Upperworld is very different from the Midworld and Underworld below. The Underworld feels heavier and more contained to me. When I am in the Upperworld, things are very light and sometimes abstract. This is the world of the stars, planets, and universal energies that humans are just now beginning to understand. The Upperworld is extremely vast and one can become lost easily. The Upperworld guide will help you find the places of the gods and the places of power and wisdom. He or she can give you wise counsel on how to deal with gods and spirits you have never encountered before. They can also help you avoid those dangerous places that are deep in the above worlds.

Finding your Upperworld Guide

1. Choose one of the astral exercises and travel to the World Tree.

2. Once there, make the following statement: "I wish to find my Upperworld Guide".

3. Call upon your totem animal.

4. See the trunk of the World Tree in front of you. Look up into the sky and visualize the branches of the Great Tree that go all the way up into the air, through the clouds and into outer space.

5. See yourself flying up, following the branches into the sky. Some shamans will visualize themselves transforming into a bird to fly up into the Upperworld. When you arrive in the Upperworld, what do you see? What does the landscape look like?

6. Keep the intention to find your Upperworld Guide in your mind. Begin to explore the Upperworld. Ask your totem animal to show you the way.

7. Trust your intuition. Look for people and animals along the way

and ask them if they are your Upperworld Guide. If not, ask them to point out the direction in which you can find your guide.

8. Once you find an entity who is a likely candidate to become your Upperworld Guide, ask if he or she is willing to help you navigate the Upperworld. If the answer is "no," the entity is not your guide and you should keep looking. If the answer is "yes," ask for his or her name. Then ask your Guide if there is anything he or she would like in return. If the request is reasonable and you are able and willing to do it, then by all means do it. If not, graciously explain why you cannot meet the request.

9. Know that you can call upon your Upperworld Guide each time you enter the Upperworld.

10. Come back to the Middle World the way you came. Then open your eyes and journal about your experiences.

When you are traveling to the Upperworld it is important to meet your totem in the Middleworld then begin your journey up the word tree to meet with your Upperworld guide. From there, you may travel into the vastness of the heavens and the Universe itself.

2 Creation

Epic Of Creation (Mesopotamia)

Before the gods there was the great Waters

Tiamat, the Ocean and Aspu, the fresh waters

Through their mingling came the primals gods Lahmu and Lahamu

Through them came Anshar and Kishar, and through them, Anu

Anu bore the wise and mighty Ea

Ea wanted to stir Tiamat, the first goddess

The god Ea caused the Ocean Goddess to be hit with great waves

This offended Tiamat and she grew very angry

Her husband, Aspu, plotted to kill his children

But Ea heard of this and killed him first!

During the quiet time of peace,

Ea had a son, Marduk

Anshar, king of the gods was so pleased with Marduk

He gave him the four winds

Ea saw an advantage, he told his little son

To play and send waves through the ocean,

Angry , was the great Tiamat,

Tiamat would have no more

She created a powerful army from her venom and they began to number

In fear, Ea went to his father, but Anshar could not help him

Ea knows his son is powerful and could defeat Tiamat

If he he has the full power of the gods

Ea held council with the elder gods and told of his plan

Marduk knows he can stop the Ocean, but he needs more power

The Elder gods agree to relinquish their power to Marduk

So Marduk may have victory

The Elder gods give Marduk all their magick

It is he who now holds the fates of the Universe

It is he who now can rule time and space

Marduk faced Tiamat and her armies on the battlefield

He challenges her to single combat!

With magick, given to him from his grandfather

He forces the four winds into her mouth and her body

Her belly filled with wind,

Marduk shoot the arrow that pierced her gut

Tiamat fell

Her power over the Universe was now his to take

With his new mighty magick

He split Tiamat in two

The first half he threw up and made the heavens, the world of gods

The second half he made the world of earth and stone

They gods made him their ruler

Then, Marduk went to the heavens

And made the stars and planets and the sun and moon

He then made himself into a constellation

The beginning of all things is one of the most profound of all the mysteries. From the moment we begin to question our surroundings and our Universe, one of the first questions we may ask is "Where did everything come from?" Every culture and every religion has an origin or creation story. Some of the stories are very elaborate myths of how the gods came together to create the Universe. Other cultures simply say that it was made by God. For the human consciousness, the understanding of how and why everything came to be may help understand the self. We want there to be a greater reason for our existence. We want to know that we are all part of a Great Divine Purpose. Perhaps this will make each of us, individually, feel special and that we have a greater purpose to our lives.

Creation stories give us a small insight of whom the gods are and why they created the cosmos, earth, and human beings. We cannot begin to understand all the reasons fully, but we may catch a fleeting glimpse as to why. Creation stories are also told to explain the energies and forces of the earth and cosmos. Before the ancient peoples knew of science, they had the myths of their priests and shamans. It was the shaman who had the knowledge and the magical powers to see the spirits and gods. It was believed that they could ask the spirits and gods directly how the Universe was made. With this information, perhaps we could find the deeper meaning of our lives.

The important thing to know about creation myths is that they are not to be taken literal. They are stories that were invented long ago to teach us about the Universe and how the cosmos works in harmony. In the world of myth, time and space is not necessarily a constant. It is believed that myths play out in the past, present, and future. The stories are always unfolding before us. It turns out that, scientifically, there is truth to this. In quantum-physics, it is said that everything that ever was and everything that is ever going to be is happening right here and now. To add to your confusion, physicists say that there are also multiple timelines with multiple outcomes to each decision that we make. What this means is that our decisions create multiple timelines with each decision. Think of it like the branches of a tree. We start with a base and something comes up that leads us to make a decision. The base splits off into two timelines. It is said that there are multiple "selves" that live out each choice we make, our do not make, and therefore we have multiple selves with multiple outcomes in multiple time lines. We could contemplate this for our whole lives and never fully grasp this concept. For our purposes here, just understand that legends and myths are constantly playing out. Even now, it is possible that more myths with the gods are unfolding. We just have yet to discover them.

Each culture may have a completely different creation myth to explain the origin of the Universe. Some of the themes are familiar in each myth, but how creation came to be is entirely original to each culture. One explanation of this is just simply what they believe. If you believe your gods to have certain abilities, then they will use those abilities for creation in a way that is congruent to their personalities, hopes, fears, and desires. Another reason for the differences is their environment. The creation of the world to the people of a desert culture will be quite different to those who live in a jungle environment. It is also how they observe nature. To people of the desert, life is harsh and unforgiving. There is not a lot of rest and food is scarce. The people must be creative when hunting and making homes. The gods of these people may be harsh and unforgiving. Therefore, the creation myth may be harsh and unforgiving. The important thing to understand when learning and understanding myths from culture to culture is that each of these peoples believed their gods to have a divine purpose for all things. By observing their environment, perhaps the gods would reveal a little of this purpose bit by bit.

The Big Bang

The Universe, as we understand it, began with what we call "The Big Bang". Over 14 billion years ago the universe came into existence. It began from an explosion so hot and so enormous that scientist can only theorize the temperatures. The greatest cosmic event is thought to have manifested from nothing, but perhaps a single point. It is believed that the temperature from the big bang reached 10 thousand million degrees and began cooling soon after the magnificent explosion. This amazing force is thought to have been symmetrical. Meaning, that it is was one force soaring into the nothingness of space at equal temperature, speed, and force. As the energy of the big bang soared into outer space, the force of energy began to splinter into four parts. The first force to break away from the first energy is gravity. The Universe as it was at that point cooled even further. It is here the elements of Hydrogen and Helium would make up most of the universe.

About 380,000 years after the big bang, the Universe cooled enough for atoms to form and in 1 billion years after the big bang the galaxies and quasars began to form. A few billion years after this, the stars and planets formed as we know them today. When the energies of the big bang were forming, or rather breaking away from the first force they formed four energies: gravity, electromagnetic force, strong nuclear force, and weak nuclear force.

In Alchemical Magick it is taught that all things in the Universe is made up of the four elements. Air, Fire, Water, and Earth. Fire is the male principle and is hot and dry. It transforms one thing into another and is very active. Water is the female principle and is cool and wet. It is cooling. Air is the combination of Fire and Water and is hot and moist. It is expansive. Earth is a combination of fire, water, and air and is cold and dry. It is they physical manifestation of all the elements.

Gravity is the force that attracts things together. The funny thing is is that scientist understand how gravity works but they do not understand what it is exactly other than it is a "force". Gravity is what keeps us connected to the earth. It is the force from the earth that keeps the moon in it's "gravitational field" and the force from the sun that keeps the planets rotating around it. It is also the force that keeps our Milky Way galaxy continually spiraling. We can see how this force may correspond to the element of fire.

Electromagnetic force is the second force. It is made up of electric and magnetic force. It contains electrons and quarks. This energy is what aids us in our modern world of technology. This force corresponds to the element of air.

Weak nuclear force is the third force. This force is made up of electrons and neutrinos. This energy is what makes radioactivity. What happens with this force is that the nucleus of the atom will break down because it is weak and cannot hold the atom together. This force corresponds to the element of water.

Strong nuclear force is the fourth force. This force is what hold atoms together. The energy here forms the elements in the Universe. Strong nuclear force literally makes up our physical reality. This force corresponds to the element of earth.

It is interesting to me that the combination of weak and strong nuclear force is what makes up light.

Parallel Universes and Other dimensions

Where is heaven, one might ask? Where are the gods and spirits that myths talk about? This is a question that humanity has been asking itself since the beginning of time. In some religions the priests simply say to have faith. In paganism and magick we do not simply have *faith* that the other worlds and the gods exist. We have the power to journey and see for ourselves. In magical philosophy, we say that the spirits live on another plane of existence. This may be the astral or spiritual planes. Since we are in a physical body we cannot easily see this plane and interact with its inhabitants because we are not of spirit. I personally enjoy taking a more scientific view. There are many energies in the universe that we cannot see. There are radio waves, gamma rays, x-rays, and so forth. None of which we can see with the naked eye. None of these energies were detected until the last 100 years or so. If scientist are discovering new energies then is it possible that the gods are energies that we have not yet been able to detect? Yes! Of course!

In Shamanism, we teach that there are many worlds to discover. There are the ten sephiroths of the Kabbalistic philosophy, there are the nine worlds of the great Nordic Tree Yggdrasil, and the many heavens of the Greek, Egyptian, Maya, Shinto and many other religions. I was taught as a child (I grew up Christian) that there was only one heaven and all other religions were wrong. This is simply not the case. There are indeed many other heavens in the Upperworld. Scientist have theories of other parallel universes that live near our own. There is the "Inflation Theory" that says that the energies that began our universe with the Big Bang have the ability to do it again, multiple times, to create other universes. We call this the *Multiverse*. How this happens is that somehow the energies can gather and push out other universes. In his book *Parallel Worlds: A Journey Through Creation, Higher Dimensions, and The Future of the Cosmos,* Michio Kaku says, "Imagine blowing soap bubbles into the air. If we blow hard enough, we see that some soap bubbles split in half and generate new soap bubbles. In the same way, universes may be continually giving birth to new universes. In this scenario, big bangs have been happening continually."

Another theory says that there is perhaps the birthing of other universes from black holes. If we remember the theory of the Big Bang, an immeasurable amount of energy came from some unexplained place and scattered an intense amount of heat/energy into nothingness until it cooled enough to form atoms. But where did this heat/energy come from? Some scientist speculate that perhaps it come from a giant black hole. How black holes work is that the force of gravity is so high that it traps everything, including light, into it. The intense gravity will allow nothing to escape. Not even light. So going with this theory, if light cannot escape the gravitational pull, than most likely, nothing else can either. No one knows what happens to the light and energy on the other side of the black hole. There is a theory that says, perhaps, on the other side of the black hole is an enormous spout of energies that shoots out a gigantic pillar of light and energy. However, another theory says that perhaps it collects so much energy that it creates another Big Bang to create another universe.

It is theorized that each of these different universes will have their own unique laws of physics. Some may be similar to our own universe, while others may be completely opposite. Imagine a universe where men can shoot lightning from their hands and women can use their energies to bring crops forth from the earth itself. In *Parallel Worlds,* Michio Kaku goes on to say, "The multiverse idea is appealing, because all we have to do is assume that spontaneous breaking occurs randomly. No other assumptions have to be made. Each time a universe sprouts off another universe, the physical constants differ from the original, creating new laws of physics. If this is true, then an entire new reality to can emerge from each."

There is also the theory of another dimension. In older sci-fi novels another special dimension would be called the Fourth Dimension, however scientist view the fourth dimension as *time,* therefore, it would be more correctly called the *Fifth Dimension.* In this theory, any being in the third dimension (where we live now) would be unaware of the comings and goings of the fifth dimension. What happens is the beings from the fifth who would come to the third dimension would not resonate with the energies of the third dimension. Light would pass beneath or around him and he would not be visible to our human eye. He would seem like a spirit. One of the examples that Michio Kaku uses is that imagine the world of a fish living under water. Their whole world is the sea. They are unaware that a more "advanced" civilization is living just above them. We can see the fish, but unless we dive underwater, they cannot see us.

I think these theories are very interesting when they try to explain the existence of higher beings. Perhaps the life forms that we think are angels or gods are more correctly beings that live in the fifth dimension or a parallel universe. In quantum and astrophysics it is theorized the laws maybe different in parallel universes. So perhaps in other universes, men and women can fly and lift mountains. Perhaps they can turn into showers of gold or even move whole galaxies with simply a passing thought. All very interesting ideas. Are they true? Perhaps. Perhaps not. I encourage anyone who is interested in the magick of the Upperworld to journey into the heavens as well as study quantum and astrophysics. After all, magick is an art *and* a science.

Egyptian Creation

A void. Nun. The primordial waters. The void.
Swimming through the dark waters was the great serpent
A mighty spark formed within the serpent.
Amun.
Amun could not remain as he was.
Amun metamorphosed into the great scarab Kheprer
The Becoming One
Wrapped in the great serpent, Amun released himself.
From the death of the serpent came the first reed
That takes root in Nun, the void
The first light, the primordial flicker of light, Ra
Takes to the reed.
Ra, is Atum in the form of light.

Atum, with penis erect places his seed into his hand then

In act of birth, places it into his mouth.

From this act of creation

Birthed the God Shu and the goddess Tefnut

Shu is the universe of space who forever loves

Tefnut who is forever within his space as the beginning

Of formation, but is not formation.

Through their love, their union

Came Nut and Geb

Nut, the goddess of the starry night

Geb, the God of the fertile earth itself

Born together

Embraced in each other's arms

But, for creation to flourish, Geb and Nut must

Be set apart

Their father, Shu, separated them, much to their sorrow

So land and sky could form.

For here and forever do Geb and Nut

Look longingly into each other's eyes

Together yet separate.

From this came

Osiris

Isis

Seth

Nephthys

For the night sky is the place of the gods.

Kabbalistic Creation Theory

I do not think we can have a book about the Upperworld without talking about the Kabbalistic Tree of Life. I know several people who are witches or who walk a shamanistic path and say that there is no reason for them to have a working knowledge of Kabbalah. I beg to differ. I do not think a shaman or a witch has to be an expert in the magical applications of the Kabbalah, but there is a whole magical universe out there that has God names, archangels, and angelic orders that can help you on your magical path and spiritual evolution. I was always taught that a good magician, witch, etc. has a working knowledge of several traditions. I will admit that I am biased because I do think it is great fun to travel up and down the Tree of Life and gain access to ancient knowledge through the entities and intelligences who live there. For the purposes of this book, I will not go into great detail about the Tree of Life and all of its magical formulas and incantations. There are several wonderful books such as Donald Michael Kraig's *Modern Magick: Twelve Lessons in the High Magical Arts* and Lon Milo Duquette's *The Chicken Qabalah of Rabbi Lamed Ben Clifford* that I highly recommend on this subject. For the purposes of this book I will give you the basics from a more of a shamanistic or Traditional Witchcraft point of view. Excited yet?

I first discovered the Kabbalistic Tree of Life when I lived in New York City in 2000. I will admit I bought the book simply because it said *Modern Magick*. I thumbed through it at the bookstore and none of it made sense at the time so I figured I would buy and figure it out as I went. I began carefully studying each lesson and found that I was learning energy summoning and control at a much faster rate than I had been with the available books on witchcraft at the time. As excited I was on the subject, I was confused about how I could use ceremonial magick and witchcraft at the same time. But I studied it nonetheless. When I began formal magical training with Matthew Ellenwood in 2001, part of our training was ceremonial magick and the Tree of Life. I purposed the question that I was conflicted about. Lucky for me, Matthew was also a Kabbalist as well as a shaman and a witch. His answer was that in Kabbala, we travel to each of the sephiroth, called path workings, using similar techniques that shamans and witches use when they are are journeying. In my research and study on Traditional Witchcraft, witches would use many foreign techniques and magical formula that travelers would teach them in order to obtain their magical goals. This, to me, made perfect sense. So, we are able to incorporate Kabbalistic teachings and principles into our shamanistic tool box.

The Tree of Life

There was no beginning, no time, no space, there was only no-thing. That which created all·things was not anything at all, but yet, it was all, which was no-thing.

The Source of all things was and is limitless, without boundary. The limitless became the limitless light. The source, the creator, wanted to know itself. Creator wanted to move beyond limitless powers and know itself in a deeper way. Creator wanted to evolve and understand its own complexities and have the ability to evolve.

The Creator formed energy to the first sephiroth, Keter, the Crown of the Universe. This was the first. But still Creator was alone, but was more aware of itself in its entirety. Creator wanted to know more about itself so the divine energy formed a likeness of itself, but was not itself, the second sephiroth was formed, Chochmah. The Divine Father was formed. What wisdom will the universe have? Oh, the magick it will have. From the two sephiroth's formed three, Binah, the Divine Mother.

With Understanding, She took into herself all the potentiality of Chochmah and began the formation of the universe. The Source, The Divine Father, and The Divine Mother existed. This is the God and the Goddess.

There is a great abyss that separates the divine triad. This abyss is of great chaos and is a portal to the darkness of the Underworld, it is a great veil that keeps those away from Divine Triad who are not ready to experience the holiest of holies. Even through the abyss, the power of the divine Triad, cannot be contained. The reflection of three forms below. The energies of Binah forms the fourth sephiroth, Chesed, the order of the universe. The Mercy of the universe is wonderful, but what is a universe with no power? From this, the fifth sephiroth is formed, Geburah, the Strength of the universe. Now the universe is moving ever so quickly into formation. Keter, the source of all things is not understandable to the universe, but perhaps its reflection of itself below the abyss. Yes, a sephiroth to balance order and power, Beauty it will be. From the fifth sephiroth formed the sixth, Tiphereth, the divine son and balance of the Universe.

Yet again, the universe must create itself from a reflection of itself. A universe must be filled with the Victory of love. The sixth sephiroth created the seventh. Oh, how holy this new universe will be, for nothing is more sacred than love. But, love can ever expand into chaos if not for the Splendor of logic. Then, the eighth sephiroth is formed. The universe is magnificent. Is it perfect? Or can it be perfect in its imperfections. The Foundation of the universe. The eternal force that purifies the energies of the higher sephiroths to the physical world. Yesod, the ninth sephiroth. Yet again a reflection of a reflection. From Keter to Tiphareth, to Yesod. Then finally the kingdom of the divine, Malkuth. The formation and evolution of the Universe is complete.

Wisdom of the Shaman

When we work with the shamanic tree of life we will make connections with many spirits, gods, and ancestors. There are many higher beings in the Upperworld that are very willing to help us upon our path. That being said, there are gods and spirits that can literally show us the creation of the Universe. I believe that the ancient shamans of each culture journeyed to the Upperworld to understand the creation of the Universe. In magical thought, all time and space are here and now. Everything that ever was, is, and will be are unfolding simultaneously in the astral plane. This is one of the reasons people who are clairvoyant can see the past, present, and the future. Using this same philosophy, the shaman is able to journey into the deepest past and observer creation. Each shaman from each culture may observe creation a bit differently. They will see things unfold in their cultural context. So for the Egyptians they may see creation come out of the ocean or river. For the Nordic people of the north, they will see creation come from fire and ice. I highly recommend that you take some time and journey to the Upperworld to witness creation. Ask your Upperworld Guide to take you to the place where you can observe creation. I have listed below a few poetic descriptions of creation from a pagan point of view. Spend some time journeying through the different creation myths so that you can get a better understanding. You can read the poems below into a voice recorder and play them as you journey. Or you can simply read them and then journey to the the above. You may not see the creation of each myth exactly as they are written. I have taken a few poetic liberties simply for the sake of art and writing. Also, you will perceive the energies through your own psychic lense. Meaning the energies will be filtered through your own cultural context and your own hopes, fears, desires, and prejudices. I encourage you to write down your own observation of creation. Tell the story how you see it!

Vishnu Enlightens Brahma (Hindu)

Brahma, the god of creation
Became aware of himself to himself
He was god and yet he did not remember
Creating himself to himself
He noticed that he sat on a grand cosmic lotus
Upon further inspection,
He saw that the stalk of the lotus
Came from the navel of a greater being than he
In amazement, Brahma saw that this great being
Meditated on the coils of a great serpent
"Who are you?" Brahma asked
"I am he who takes the Universe into myself
For the Universe is me and unto me
It shall return. I am Narayana. I am Vishnu"
Narayana was kind and powerful
But he was in a state of mysterious meditation
Where he would always remain
So, he whispered the Vedas into the ear of Brahma
Through this, Brahma became enlightened
Brahma knew it was his dharma
To create all things in the cosmos

The Lay of the Beginning (Nordic)

In the beginning there was no life
There was no earth and no stars

The north contained Niflheim, the world of frost

The South had Muspelheim, the world of fire

Between these worlds lay nothingness, a great void

Ginnungagap

These worlds rolled into each other through the void

The fires of Muspellheim melted the ice of Niflheim

From the melted ice came the giant, Ymir

There was also the great cow, Audhumla, who came from the ice

Audhumla, the great cow, licked the melting ice

From this, Buri was released from an icy prison

From Ymir were born his children, the giants

Bori married one of the giants and had a son, Bor

Bor married Bestla, another giant and together they had

Odin, Vile, and Ve

The three brothers knew they had to kill Ymir

To create the worlds

After Ymir was killed, the three brothers

From his blood was the oceans

From his flesh soil was made

From his bones were mountains and stones

The sky is the inside of his skull

And the stars and planets

Sparks from the fires of Muspellhiem

Pangu Creates the Universe (Chinese)

Before everything ever was

There was a great cosmic chicken egg

Inside the egg the mighty god, Pangu grew

He grew to be very tall and very mighty

While inside the egg

He separated heaven and earth

The white was heaven and the yolk was earth

Pangu, grew to be very very tall

Until one day he broke the cosmic egg

Allowing heaven and earth to spill forth

In the east, he saw two shining sisters; one of silver and one of gold

He asked the golden one to light up the day

and the silver one to light up the night

The golden sister was very shy

and did not want people to stare at her

So silver sister gave her golden pins

To poke the eyes of those who stared

Pangu became so great he began to transform

His breath became the winds

His voice the thunder

His body created the mountains and the fields

While his blood created the oceans and rivers

and his hair and beard became the stars and planets

The Birth of the Gods (Greco-Roman)

No one quite remembers the very beginning

Not even the gods, themselves, remember

How the firsts became the firsts

There was nothing at all,

but then came the first God, Chaos.

Some say Chaos was hatched out of a magnificent cosmic egg

Some say the first God simply...was

No one remembers

Along with Chaos came Mother Earth

Next came Tartarus

who was to dwell in a hidden place within the great Mother

Then came desire-Eros is his name

Chaos began to bare children

Whose names where Darkness and Night

Night, herself, then bore two children, by the love of Chaos

There names are Day and Brightness

Mother Earth gave birth to the Sky

who became equal to her power and magic

She loved him with a love

that could not be matched by the gods even to this day

Through their union, their child Ocean was created

The Union of Earth and Sky

Created the elder race of gods

From them the gods we know now.

Kronos and his sons and daughters

But what of Night?

What gods were created

From this strange and wondrous goddess?

Night was a powerful goddess and needed

No God to help her create her children

From herself she bore her dark children

Their names are Fate, Death, Dreams, Sleep, Nemesis, Retribution, Strife

And many more

For as the children of Mother Earth

Sustains the lives of the gods and humans

The children of Night challenge them

And teach them how to fall and yet rise.

The Shamanic Way To Create Our Universe

Shamans from all over the world have known that we have the power to co-create our Universe into being. It is through our thoughts, emotions, desires, and fears that our environment comes into manifestation. In both Hinduism and Buddhism, it is believed our physical world is the world of illusion or *maya*. What this means is that our physical world is shaped by all of us depending on our conscience and subconscious thoughts while the world of spirit is constant. When we perform acts of magick, we are shaping our world with the help of the spirits, gods, and ancestors. The Law of Attraction states that anything you are focusing on will come into being in your environment. This is the basis of sympathetic magick. In this type of magick, anytime we use an object to represent something else and manipulated it to our Will, our desire MUST come into being. By using magical objects such as medicine or mojo bags, stones, herbs, colors, poppets, etc we are using the law of attraction to obtain our desires.

When we connect our spirit and soul to the natural flow of the Universe, we can shape the world for the betterment of all. There are stories of Buddhist monks who sit on the mountain top dreaming the world into being by meditating and bringing the biorhythms of the world into harmony. Using this same logic, we can shape our lives in accordance to our desires. In order to do this, we must begin to the process of understanding ourselves. We must understand our fears, our hopes, our dreams, and what it is what we really want. It is vital that we understand ourselves because we often bring into manifestation that part of ourselves we do not understand. How many times have you seen someone try to succeed in careers, love, and health only to self sabotage themselves? They want to succeed but some force always send them back a few steps. That force is the part of their mind that does not want them to succeed or is afraid of success on some level.

When we are connected to the natural forces of the ebb and flow of the Universe, we will have a better chance of succeeding. When I teach this philosophy to my students I am often asked, "What if two people are wishing to manifest two opposing things, who gets their wish?" The answer is quite simple. The one who is more connected to their environment and is self aware. Self aware does not mean perfect. It means they understand what their hopes and fears are. They understand the ebb and flow of the earth, moon, sun, and planets. They are aware of the power of the stars and the gods themselves. When we are connected to our Divine Will our desires become congruent with the natural flow of the Universe.

Creating Our Universe

1. Spend time in meditation contemplating what is your Divine Will.

2 .Journey to the gods, angels, and ascended beings to aide you in discovering how best you can serve Spirit.

3. Learn the lessons of the planets and stars and the spirits that rule and aide them. These beings can teach you valuable lessons and help you learn about your strengths and weaknesses.

4. Learn from the challenges in your life. What lessons are these challenges trying to teach you? How are they making you stronger? What are your fears? How can you overcome them?

5. Seek the betterment of the self physically, emotionally, spiritually, and mentally.

6. In meditation, visualize your world as you like it. You must connect mentally, emotionally, and spiritually to the Universe to create a physical outcome. Go deep to the core of your spirit; the part of yourself that creates with the divine authority of the gods themselves.

3
The Heavens

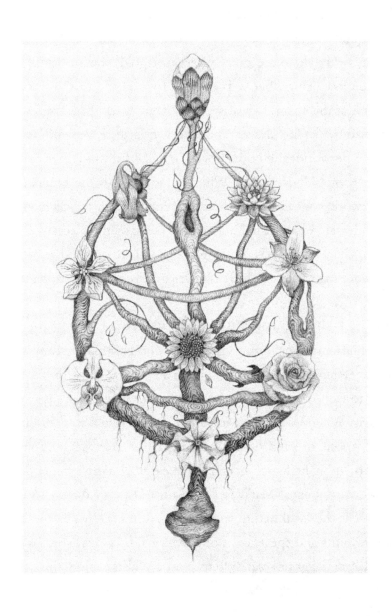

The spiritual realm of the heavens holds much power and healing. It is where we find many gods and spiritual beings. The energies of the heavens tend to be more "ethereal" and abstract compared to the lower worlds. For this reason, I find it very helpful to have mapping points that I can visit when I need. When we read mythology, it is filled with descriptions of the land of the gods and many other beings that can be found in the Upperworld. There are great palaces of gold, shining lands of spirit, and rainbow beings that help guide our world and the Universe. When we look at the cosmological symbol of the world tree, we see that the divine source of life (the sun) pours down to the leaves and branches of tree (Upperworld) and nourishes the trunk (Midworld) then flows down to the roots (Underworld). When we journey to the branches of the Upperworld we can have a direct experience with the divine nature of the Universe. I have listed below only some of the places you can visit in your shamanic travels. These places listed are only to get you started. There are many places of the Upperworld yet to be discovered.

Space, Planets, and Far Off Galaxies

Shamanic journeying through the Upperworld has many advantages other than meeting the gods and angels. You can travel to distant parts of space to explore things that the human race may never get a chance to discover. When we are traveling in the astral plane, we are not bound by speed, space, or even time. We can get to where we are going at the speed of thought; literally a blink of the eye. You can explore the terrain of Mercury, Venus, Mars, Jupiter, Saturn, and so forth. You are also able meet the local nature spirits that live there. Just as the earth has nature spirits and spirits of mountains, winds, and storms, so does the other planets in our solar system. You can also explore the end of the

Milky Way galaxy as well as other galaxies. It is easier if you already have an idea where you want to explore such as the Andromeda Galaxy.

When you are exploring the planets and deep space, you will discover strange spacial phenomenon and energies. Remember, it is sometimes better for us to have a better understanding of the new energies we encounter if we allow them to be personified as human-like in our minds. For example, if I were traveling through Jupiter's atmosphere, instead of trying to figure out exactly what energetic phenomenon I was encountering, I might ask the energy to appear into a human shape so I can have a dialogue with the energy. This way we can have a direct conversation with what is happening. This is a similar technique that ancient shamans used when speaking with the four winds, the rising sun, or the thunderous storms.

Astral Library/Akashic Records

The Astral Library can be a very important resource on your spiritual and magical path. It has the ability to show you the past, present, and future as well as a vast magical knowledge on many topics. The Astral Library has been in existence since the beginning of time. It holds all the records of the Universe as well as personal records of each person that has ever lived, is living, or will live in the future. It also contains the records of everyone's past lives. It is sometimes referred to as the *Akashic Records*. Akasha in Sanskrit means *ether* or *spirit* which is sometimes used as another word for astral. The Astral Library appears as a vast library in the Otherworlds full of books. There are many floors to the library. So many floors that no one actually knows the exact size of it. Each level has many bookshelves filled with every book imaginable on every subject. Space and time have no meaning here. You are in between the worlds and you can access anything. The drawback is that you have to have the ability and willingness to "see" what the books have to offer. Just like in any magical teaching, you cannot see what you are not ready to see and you cannot learn what you are not ready to learn.

The Astral Library may be useful in helping you discover what your life purpose is. Many of us may feel lost because we feel we have no purpose in life. We quickly become bored with the humdrum of everyday responsibilities of going to work, paying bills, and doing it all over again each day for the rest of our lives. We yearn for something more. The library can help you with this. Yes, you can also learn about our past lives, but learning about our past lives can distract us from our current purpose in life.

The Library has teachers and library keepers, or Astral Librarians, who are spirits who can assist you in our search to find the book you are looking for. They are very friendly spirits who take great joy in assisting you. They are well versed in every subject matter can easily direct you to the right level and the right bookshelf.

I encourage every magical practitioner to spend time in the Astral Library. I use it for a variety of reasons. Some of which include:

1. Learning magick and healing

2. Cultivating a vocational trade

3. Seeing my personal past, present, future

4. Seeing someone else's past, present, and future for healing.

5. Discovering the Divine Purpose of myself or others upon their request.

To Access The Astral Library

1. You may lie down or sit up with your spine straight in a chair.

2. Take a breath and on the inhale, draw in the connection you have to the Universe, on the exhale allow the mind to relax. Take another breath, on the inhale draw in the connection you have to the Universe, on the exhale allow the emotions to relax. Take another breath, on the inhale draw in the connection you have with the Universe, on the exhale allow the body to relax.

3. Allow yourself to go into a trance state.

4. In your mind, have the intention to journey to the Astral library. The Library will take the shape that feels right to you. The Library is in the energy world so it will be shaped by your thoughts. Allow this to be so and know it is right for you.

5. Take a moment to see the vastness of the Astral Library. When you are ready ask for an Astral Librarian to help you find the book on the subject you are looking for.

6. Once you are directed to the book open it and allow whatever happens to happen. Just like with scrying, you may see vivid pictures and scenes or you may get thoughts or a "knowing". You may even get symbols and metaphors. Be open to the experience.

7. When you are ready, thank the Astral Librarian for their help and return to everyday waking consciousness.

8. Journal Your experience and your findings.

Astral Places of Healing

The Upperworld has many places of healing. The cosmos is filled with an abundance of energy that we are able to use for wellbeing and balance of our daily lives. Science is discovering many cosmic energies such as gamma waves and subatomic particles that come from deep space. As magical practitioners, we know science discovers things that magicians have known for thousands of years. There are many places in the cosmos that have regenerative powers. I have often perceived these places as vast worlds of color and healing. When journeying to places of healing, ask your Upperworld guide to show you these beautiful places. There are many that are yet undiscovered that can help you return to balance and health.

Native American Above World

In many Native American tribes, the world above is the place of the Thunder Beings who grant shamans great healing power. It is also a place of the luminary beings of the star people. This is the world of Grandfather Sun and Grandmother Moon. It has been described as glasslike and shimmering. There are many tribes who live in the Upperworld. This is also the place that contains the Milky Way. The Milky Way is believed to the be magical road that leads the ancestors to the world of the divine. It is easy to journey to this world, simply find a star and journey up.

Babylonian Heaven

The highest level of the Babylonian Upperworld is the dwelling place of Anu, the creator and father of the gods. He is omnipotent and far to advanced for human understanding. He gives his energies to the gods below. This level of Heaven is made from red stone with small patches of red and black.

The middle heaven is the dwelling place of the gods and goddesses. These beings have direct contact with humans and influence the life, death, and rebirth process of the earth and human wants and needs. This heaven is made from blue stone.

The lowest heaven is the dwelling place of the stars, planets, and sun and moon. This heaven is influenced by the gods in the middle heaven so they can give messages to humans on the earth below. This heaven is made of clear stones. You can see through it to the stone bottom of the middle heaven in the daytime sky. The Babylonians believed that this is why the sky appears to be blue.

Egyptian Otherworld

The Egyptian Upperworld was located in the body of the starry sky goddess, Nut. Nut is the spiritual aspect of the of the Universe, while her consort, Geb, is the earth and the physical universe. The Otherworld was located within the body of Nut, or more closely to another dimension inside Nut, the sky goddess. This realm was called the Duat. The Duat contained the Egyptian Underworld, but it also contained the Upperworld, or world of the gods. It may be a bit confusing at first to know that the Underworld and Upperworld were in the same place. It is more that they were in different planes of existence in the Duat. The Egyptians believed that the physical world is a mirror image of the world of the gods; therefore, the world of the gods would look like Egyptian cities. When traveling to the Upperworld you may see palaces and pyramids of gold and many beautiful sculptures of the gods. The sky is full of stars. Just as the earth, there are rivers, fields, sand dunes and many other things. The land of reeds, called Aaru, is where the souls of the dead dwell once completed the ceremony of the weighing of the Ma'at's feather.

Muspellheim

In Nordic cosmology, Muspellheim is the world of fire. In the beginning of all things there existed two worlds; Muspellheim, the world of fire, and Niflheim, the land of ice. These two worlds collided to create the nine worlds of Nordic lore. Muspellheim was originally thought to be part of the Midworld, but some modern Heathens have come to believe that the first fires would have to be in the very top of Yggdrasil, the world tree. This world is made of fire, ash, and stone. I think it is very beautiful in its own right and holds many magical mysteries. It contains many fire giants who are fiery and wild in nature. They are governed by the ruler of that world, Surt. In mythology, Surt will help bring upon the fiery last days of the Nordic gods. Exploring this world will help you understand the greater magick of fire, illumination, creation, and the fires of the spirit. Remember to treat the fire giants respectfully or you may get "burned".

Asgard

In Nordic cosmology, Asgard is the world of the gods and is located in the Upperworld. It is described in mythology as being at the very top of the world tree, but, again, some modern Heathens have places Asgard as below Muspellheim. This is the world of all the famous Nordic gods such as Odin, Thor, Frigg, Freyr and Freya, Njord, and many other gods. One of the most recognizable places in the Asgard is Valhalla, the great hall of Odin's warrior dead. Heathen's believe that when one falls in battle, their spirit will be taken by the Valkyries, the winged goddesses who serve Odin, to Valhalla. Valhalla is a great hall for the warrior dead who eat, drink, and fight each other all day long. If they fall, they are revived to do it all over again. Each of the gods have a hall in Asgard and there are many things to explore in this world. It is said that the only way to Asgard is through the rainbow bridge, Bifrost, However I have found that once you know where you are going, you no longer need the bridge. Just as the gods may appear to us in modern attire, I have found so, too does the dwelling places of the gods becomes modern. I love the modern take of Asgard in Marvel's movie, *Thor*. I find it beautiful and close to how I have seen Asgard in my travels.

The Greek Olympus

One of the most famous Upperworld places is Olympus. This is located on Mount Olympus in Greece and is home to many of the Greco-Roman gods. When we look at the actual mountain it may look like an ordinary mountain, but viewed with our psychic senses we can see the beautiful home of the Greek gods that has many Grecian styled temples, buildings, and monuments. I have found that the residence of Olympus are used to astral visitors but it is always better to be announced. When journeying to this wonderful place, ask your Upperworld guide to announce and show you around. If your patron and matron are Greco-Roman, you can simply ask your gods to show you Olympus.

Kabbalistic Tree of life

One of the most powerful experiences of the modern day shaman is to journey through the ten spheres of the Kabbalistic Tree of Life. A lot of witches and shamans may be turned off by the notion of exploring and studying the Tree of Life because of of its monotheistic implications, but it is, indeed, one of the most profound shamanic experiences you will have. Thousands of years ago, the Middle Eastern mystics and shamans had to journey to the ten sephiroths of the tree to receive their wisdom and power. I, myself, have been working with the tree shamanically for quite some time now. Yes, I was trained in the ways of ceremonial magick, the path of the magician, but my core is shamanism and witchcraft. I was able to take shamanism and apply them to the Kabbalistic teachings and magical techniques and come up with experiences that are powerful to me. I always said I prefer to light sage and be barefoot in the great magical temples.

As you explore the Tree of Life, you will meet archangels, angelic beings, and many other spirits and gods. Some of them will remain as your shamanic contacts for wisdom, power, and healing. These allies will aide you upon your spiritual quest as a shaman. The exercise below is a meditation of each of the ten sephiroths. You will learn to attune yourself to those energies and then you will journey to them. It helps to get your feet wet before plunging into the depths of your Kabbalistic journey. After you complete these first steps, you will be able to journey further and contact the angels and archangels of each of the sephiroths. As with all shamanic journeys, try not to judge or criticize your experiences. Each journey is unique to you. You may experience similar things as is described in books on the Kabbalistic tree, or you may not. This is your unique experience. This is your opportunity to learn something perhaps no one else has. After each of the journeys and meditations journal your experience, thoughts and emotions. It may help to record the day of the week, phase of the moon, and if you want to be akin to a Kabbalist, the planetary hours. There are many apps on smartphones that you can purchase that tell you the planetary hours of each day. What a wonderful modern world we live in.

To begin with, we will start with Malkuth because it is the sephiroth that we live in. From there, we will work up the tree until we reach Keter. There are some Kabbalistic books that say that the highest humans can journey is to Chesed, but I have found this to be untrue. Yes, our human minds cannot comprehend the full true nature of Binah,

Chokmah, and Keter, but we are not looking for "pure" understanding and consciousness with the divine at this point in our spiritual development. We are looking to make Upperworld contacts with angels and other beings in these sephiroths. It may help the student to understand that the sephiroths are not necessarily places, but states of being. Under each of the sephiroth's there is a godname. The god name is how the name of God manifests in that sephiroth. When we are journeying, it will help if you vibrate the godname as you ascend up the Tree of Life. There is also the archangel that "rules" the lower angels in each of the sephiroths. The archangel is the particular angel who will want to make contact with. They are very wise in magick, healing, power, and many other things. You can intone their name to call to them. There are the lesser angels that the archangel rules. The angels are very helpful as well.

Each sephiroth has a planet listing; except Keter and Chokmah. The planet resonates closely with the energies of the sephiroth, but is not the sephiroth. We list the planets because it helps us understand the energies of the emanations a little better. It is helpful to the student to study the energies of the planets and that way you will have a better idea of how the energies of the sephiroths interact with each other.

When we *intone* or *vibrate* a hebrew name we are sending the magick of our voices into the astral and spirit worlds to call upon certain energies and beings. As we have learned, the creation of the Universe came to be because The Creator introduced energy into the void or nothingness. In many creation stories, what created the Universe was sound or a voice. In the Bible, it says, "God said (Blank) and it was." We also have the AUM in Hindu and Buddhist philosophy. All energy has a vibration. Perhaps these stories of the Universe being created by the spoken word is a metaphor for these energies coming into being. We also use intonation because it helps our minds connect with specific energies or beings. In magick, it is important to anchor the energies of our intentions into something physical; in this case, our voice. For healing, we may use a poppet or a doll to help us focus on the person being healed. We may also use a talisman to contain energies that attracted our wishes. In this case, instead of a doll or talisman, we are using the power of the voice to act as a physical container for our magick and intent.

Intonation is magick. When we think of the word or words we manifest it on the mental and astral plane. As we inhale our breath, we are building up the energy. When we say the words aloud we are creating a physical catalyst for our evocation. The echo, or ringing in our temple space is the manifestation of our magick.

For example: For Malkuth, think of how we will say the word.

Breathe in the power. Intone the world like this,

"MAAAAAAALLLLLLKUUUUUUUUUUUUTTTTTTTH"

It should be loud and deliberate. No soft mantras here!!

Here are some hints to help you with pronunciation:

Ch is pronounced ccchhhhh as in Loch

I in pronounced eeeeeeee

A is pronounced aaaaahhhh

E is pronounced a as in egg

U is pronounced ooooooo

Do the best you can with pronunciations. If you do not say it "correctly" that is ok. Do the best you can. It is not about saying everything exactly but rather the intent of your mind, emotions, and your spirit that makes the magick happen.

The Ten Sephiroth of the Tree of Life

Malkuth (Kingdom)

Godname: Adonai Ha A'Retz (Lord of Earth)

Archangel: Sandalphon

Angels: Ashim (Souls of Fire)

Planet: Earth/ Four elements

Number: 10

Body Part: Feet on the earth.

Color: Citrine, Olive, Russet, Black

The four elements of earth, air, fire, and water. Final resolution of the Tree of life. The physical plane. Stability. Form. The Soul of the earth. Nature. Life and the evolution of life. The balance of all sephiroths. The crystallization or formation of the spirit into matter. The Inferior Mother.

Meditation:

Connect with the four elements of earth, air, fire, and water. Connect with all terrains of the earth; forests, mountains, prairie, desert, tundra, etc, Become aware of the astral spirits of the physical plane. How can this world help you have a healthy body? It may help to connect to Earth gods such as Pan, Gaia, Demeter, Geb, Mother Earth.

Journey:

Get into a trance space. Use one of the astral projection techniques. Once you are out of your body, see yourself in your working space. There is a door that appears before you. When you go through the door you will see the astral counterpart of the physical plane. Explore the world of Malkuth. Get to know the terrain and meet any spirits that

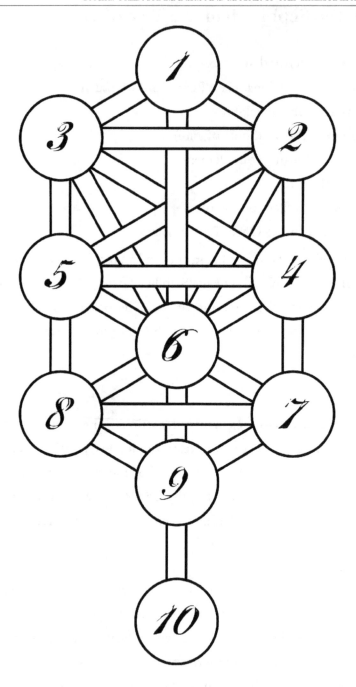

present themselves to you. When you are done, return to waking consciousness and journal your experience.

Yesod (Foundation)

Godname: Shaddai El Chai

Archangel: Gabriel

Angels: Kerubim (The Strong)

Planet: The Moon

Number: 9

Body Part: Genitals, Groin

Color: Violet

Purifies the emanations of the other sephiroth. Corrects the design of the Universe. Spiritual Experience. The understanding of the Machinery of the Universe. Akasha. Astral. Receptacle for energies of all other sephiroth. Illusion. Psychic abilities. The Unconscious. The Shadow Self. Dreams. Cycles. Tides. Hidden Magick. Rhythms.

Meditation:

Connect with the powers of the moon in her four phases; waxing, full, waning, and dark. Allow yourself to contemplate the mysteries of the moon and her magick. How can this world help your psychic awareness? It may help to connect to Gods such as Diana, Artemis, Manni, Arianhod, Grandmother Moon.

Journey:

Use one of the astral projection techniques to project from your body. See a door in front of you. See yourself in the astral counterpart of Malkuth. See the surroundings as you did when the Malkuth journey. Now, using your visualization skills, see yourself flying up to the next plane/world of Yesod. Feel the transition between the earth plane of

Malkuth to the plane of Yesod. Once in Yesod, take notice how it is different from Malkuth. How do the energies here feel? What do you see? Are there any contacts here? When you are ready, return the way you came and return to waking consciousness.

Hod (Splendor)

Godname: Elohim Tzaboath (God of Hosts)

Archangel: Michael

Angels: Beni Elohim (Sons of God)

Planet: Mercury

Number: 8

Body Part: Right Hip

Color: Orange

Consciousness. Logic and reason. Objectivity. Patterns in nature. Knowledge. Alchemy. Mental magick. Science. Language. Thought forms. The ability to concentrate the will, not will itself, but the magick to harness and direct its power. The ability to equalize opposing forces. The sphere in which form takes place. The mental ability to give abstract energies form or a symbol.

Meditation:

Connect to the ideas of logic, science, alchemy. What patterns do you see in your life and world around you? How can this world help you have better discernment? It may help to connect with gods such as Hermes, Mercury, Thoth, Coyote, Loki, Ganesha.

Journey:

Use one of the astral projection techniques to project from your body. See a door in front of you. See yourself in the astral counterpart of

Malkuth. See the surroundings as you did when the Malkuth journey. Now, using your visualization skills, see yourself flying up to the next plane/world of Yesod. Feel the transition between the earth plane of Malkuth to the plane of Yesod. Once in Yesod, take a moment to get your bearings in this world. Now, fly up and transition to the world of Hod. How do the energies here feel? Take notice of the difference between Malkuth, Yesod, and now Hod. Take a moment to explore. What do you see? Are there any contacts here? When you are ready, return the way you came and return to waking consciousness.

Netzach (Victory)

Godname: Yod Hey Vav Heh Tzabaoth (The Lord of Hosts)

Archangel: Haniel

Angels: Elohim (gods)

Planet: Venus

Number: 7

Body part: Right Hip

Color: Green

Lower octave of Chesed. Emotions. Love. Generosity. The outpouring of energetic love and honor. Devotion to the gods. Entities in this sephiroth are better contacted with dance and song. Inspiration to create art and beauty. Instincts. The life force of sexuality/ tantra that helps the devotee to rise to god consciousness. Energy that drives nature/ creation to live. Healthy sexuality in humans that promotes a healthy state of mind and harmony with body, emotions, mind, and spirit.

Meditation:

Connect to the feeling of Love, Romance, and Relationships. How do relationships enhance or harm your life? Is your sex life healthy? How can this world help you have an open heart? It may help to connect to the gods Aphrodite, Venus, Quan Yin, Freya or Freyr, Eros

Journey:

Use one of the astral projection techniques to project from your body. See a door in front of you. See yourself in the astral counterpart of Malkuth. See the surroundings as you did when the Malkuth journey. Now, using your visualization skills, see yourself flying up to the next plane/world of Yesod. Feel the transition between the earth plane of Malkuth to the plane of Yesod. Once in Yesod, take a moment to get your bearings in this world. Now, fly up and transition to the world of Netzach. How do the energies here feel? Take notice of the difference between Malkuth, Yesod, and now Netzach. Take a moment to explore. What do you see? Are there any contacts here? When you are ready, return the way you came and return to waking consciousness.

Tiphereth (Beauty)

      Godname: Yod Hey Vav Hey Aloah Va Da'ath

      Archangel: Raphael

      Angels: Malachim (Kings)

      Planet: The Sun

      Number: 6

      Body Part. Heart/Chest

      Color: Yellow or Gold

      Lower octave of Keter. Sacrificed God. Balancing force of Chesed and Geburah. Mediator. Mystical experience; that being different from psychic experience. Son of God/s. Healing. Priest who reconciles or balances the Goddess and God through devotion and within him or herself. Illumination. Christ consciousness. Buddha consciousness. Holy Guardian Angel. Harmony.

Meditation:

Connect to the concept of the Higher Self or Holy Guardian Angel. What is your view of spirit? How can this world help you tune in to your higher self in a balanced way? What healing do you need in your life? It may help to connect the gods Apollo, Asclepius, Horus, Baldar, Sunna, Grandfather Sun.

Journey:

Use one of the astral projection techniques to project from your body. See a door in front of you. See yourself in the astral counterpart of Malkuth. See the surroundings as you did when the Malkuth journey. Now, using your visualization skills, see yourself flying up to the next plane/world of Yesod. Feel the transition between the earth plane of Malkuth to the plane of Yesod. Once in Yesod, take a moment to get your bearings in this world. Now, fly up and transition to the world of Tiphereth. How do the energies here feel? Take notice of the difference between Malkuth, Yesod, and now Tiphereth. Take a moment to explore. What do you see? Are there any contacts here? When you are ready, return the way you came and return to waking consciousness.

Geburah (Severity)

Godname: Elohim Gabor

Archangel: Khamael

Angels: Seraphim (Fiery Serpents)

Planet: Mars

Number: 5

Body Part: Right Shoulder

Color: Red

Lower octave of Binah. Energy. Courage. War. Destruction. Justice. Force which breaks down things. Fear. Cuts away things that no longer benefit the cosmos or earth. Sacrifice. Divine Will. The Will of the universe that keeps things progressing. Discipline. Remover of obstacles.

Meditation:

Connect to the energies of personal Will and Divine Will. What is your great purpose for this incarnation? How do you control your personal energies and the energies around you? It may help to connect with the gods Ares, Mars, Tyr, Lugh, Seckmeth.

Journey:

Use one of the astral projection techniques to project from your body. See a door in front of you. See yourself in the astral counterpart of Malkuth. See the surroundings as you did when the Malkuth journey. Now, using your visualization skills, see yourself flying up to the next plane/world of Yesod. Feel the transition between the earth plane of Malkuth to the plane of Yesod. Once in Yesod, take a moment to get your bearings in this world. Now, fly up and transition to the world of Tiphereth. Again, allow yourself a moment to get your bearings and acclimate to Tiphereth. Now, fly up to the world of Geburah. How do the energies here feel? Take notice of the difference between Malkuth, Yesod, Tiphareth and now Geburah. Take a moment to explore. What do you see? Are there any contacts here? When you are ready, return the way you came and return to waking consciousness.

Chesed (Mercy)

Godname: El

Archangel: Tzadkiel

Angels: Chasmalim (Brilliant Ones)

Planet: Jupiter

Number: 4

Body part: Left shoulder

Color: Blue

Lower emanation of Chokmah. The loving father. Organizing the energies of the above sephiroth. Order. Place of formulation. Plane of higher consciousness of shaman/magician. The King. Leader. Obedience. Sacrifice of selfish needs to benefit the needs of the community. Virtue.

Meditation:

Connect to the energies of Leadership. How are you leading by example? Are you taking responsibility for your own life? What leadership skills do you need to learn? It may help to connect to the gods Odin, Thor, Zeus, Jupiter, Poseidon, Father Sky.

Journey:

Use one of the astral projection techniques to project from your body. See a door in front of you. See yourself in the astral counterpart of Malkuth. See the surroundings as you did when the Malkuth journey. Now, using your visualization skills, see yourself flying up to the next plane/world of Yesod. Feel the transition between the earth plane of Malchut to the plane of Yesod. Once in Yesod, take a moment to get your bearings in this world. Now, fly up and transition to the world of Tiphereth. Again, allow yourself a moment to get your bearings and acclimate to Tiphereth. Now, fly up to the world of Chesed. How do the energies here feel? Take notice of the difference between Malkuth, Yesod, Tiphareth, and now Chesed. Take a moment to explore. What do you see? Are there any contacts here? When you are ready, return the way you came and return to waking consciousness.

Binah (Understanding)

Godname: Yod Hey Vav Hey El o him

Archangel: Tzaphkiel

Angels: Aralim (Thrones)

Planet: Saturn

Number: 3

Body part: Near right ear

Color: Black

Supernal Mother. Form. Stabilizes the energy from Chokmah. The aspect of never ending energy dies into the stabilizing state of Binah. The beginning of death through form (as soon as we are born we begin our journey to death). The energies of Chokmah are always flowing until Binah contains them. Death itself. The antithesis of Keter and chokmah. The adversary. The root beginning of matter, yet not matter just yet. The vessel which contains the power. The archetype of the great cosmic womb where all life/ creation comes forth. Constriction. The Sorrowful mother. Time. Silence. Manifestation. The ability to take in information and understand.

Meditation:

Connect with the energies of Sorrowful Mother. What things have you created in your life? What have you had to leave behind for a better life? What have you had to cut away that was hindering you upon your path?

It may help to connect with the gods Chronos, Saturn, Shakti, Rhea, The Great Bear, Kali Ma, Isis

Journey:

Use one of the astral projection techniques to project from your body. See a door in front of you. See yourself in the astral counterpart of Malkuth. See the surroundings as you did when the Malkuth journey. Now, using your visualization skills, see yourself flying up to the next plane/world of Yesod. Feel the transition between the earth plane of Malkuth to the plane of Yesod. Once in Yesod, take a moment to get your bearings in this world. Now, fly up and transition to the world of Tiphereth. Again, allow yourself a moment to get your bearings and acclimate to Tiphereth. Now, fly up to the world of Binah. How do the energies here feel? Take notice of the difference between Malkuth, Yesod, Tiphareth and now Binah. Take a moment to explore. What do you see? Are there any contacts here? When you are ready, return the way you came and return to waking consciousness.

Chokmah (Wisdom)

Godname: Ya
Archangel: Ratziel
Angels: Auphanim (Wheels)
Body part: near left ear
Planet: The Zodiac
Number: 2
Color: Grey

The Big Bang. Energy pouring from the divine. Force. Divine Fire. The Supernal Father. Everything that is needed for creation spiritually, mentally, astrally, physically, all begin from this explosion of energy.

Energy without form or direction. We define it as "energy" because our understanding relates energy to this pouring out of the divine. The seed of everything of creation. Devotion. The Cosmic Phallus.

Meditation:

Connect to the energies or concept of the Big Bang. Alternately, connect to the energies of the Divine Father. What energies are pushing forward in your life? What resources are you using to accomplish your life goals? It may help to connect with the gods Tonka Shaila, Shiva, The Universe, Ra, Uranus, Chaos

Journey:

Use one of the astral projection techniques to project from your body. See a door in front of you. See yourself in the astral counterpart of Malkuth. See the surroundings as you did when the Malkuth journey. Now, using your visualization skills, see yourself flying up to the next plane/world of Yesod. Feel the transition between the earth plane of Malkuth to the plane of Yesod. Once in Yesod, take a moment to get your bearings in this world. Now, fly up and transition to the world of Tiphereth. Again, allow yourself a moment to get your bearings and acclimate to Tiphereth. Now, fly up to the world of Chokmah. How do the energies here feel? Take notice of the difference between Malkuth, Yesod, Tiphareth and now Chokmah. Take a moment to explore. What do you see? Are there any contacts here? When you are ready, return the way you came and return to waking consciousness.

Keter (The Crown)

    God name: Eh-heh-yeh (I am that I am)

    Archangel: Metatron

    Angels: Chaioth ha Qadesh (Holy Living Creatures)

Body Part: Crown, above head

Planet: The Universe or Multiverse

Number: 1

Color: White

First swirlings of creation. Not the Creator itself but the highest we as humans can understand. The Source of all things. Pure being. The one. The All. That which continues to emanate spirit. That which was before the Big Bang. The Primal Ocean in mythology. The Great Work. Primal Glory. The Root of all things.

Meditation:

Connect to the energies of being one with the Creator of all things. How is everything connected in the Universe? What is the meaning of the Source of everything to you? It may help to connect with the Source of All things, The Creator, God, Wonka Tonka, The Primordial Egg, The Primordial Waters

Journey:

Use one of the astral projection techniques to project from your body. See a door in front of you. See yourself in the astral counterpart of Malkuth. See the surroundings as you did when the Malkuth journey. Now, using your visualization skills, see yourself flying up to the next plane/world of Yesod. Feel the transition between the earth plane of Malkuth to the plane of Yesod. Once in Yesod, take a moment to get your bearings in this world. Now, fly up and transition to the world of Tiphereth. Again, allow yourself a moment to get your bearings and acclimate to Tiphereth. Now, fly up to the world of Keter.. How do the energies here feel? Take notice of the difference between Malkuth, Yesod, Tiphareth and now Keter. Take a moment to explore. What do you see?

Are there any contacts here? When you are ready, return the way you came and return to waking consciousness.

4

The Gods

The Contest For Athens (Greco-Roman)

During the reign of the king, Cecrops, there was a city with no patron deity. Both the goddess, Athena, and the god, Poseidon wanted to claim the city. They knew that whoever was the patron of the city would receive many prayers and offerings from its people. In return, the ruling god would protect the city and grant many blessings. Neither Athena nor Poseidon would give up their claim. The mighty gods of Olympus intervened and decided the two gods would have a contest. Whichever of the powerful gods created a gift that would benefit humans the most, that god shall rule.

Poseidon used his great powers of the ocean, and from the waves' sea foam sprang forth the horse! This beautiful animal would make work much easier and travel much faster. The horse was a magnificent creation indeed!

Athena used her magick and created the olive. This amazing creation could be used for many things and the gods themselves were in awe!

It was decreed that Athena was the winner! The city was names Athens and Athena would be giving the honor of the patron deity. From that day forth, Athena was a mighty goddess that granted many blessings and protected the city from enemies. The people of Athens celebrated the goddess, and she them.

Every single religion and spiritual philosophy believes in God, the gods, the Universe, or some higher power. The gods created the universe and each life, be it physical or spiritual. They are our divine mothers and fathers. Our creators. Each culture around the world has their own view on how the gods manifest themselves. It is said that god, or the gods, created humans in their own image. This is why the gods, more or less, appear to us in a human like form. But the gods are more than this. They are a product of The Source of all things. The gods, too, were created. They have power over life and death, creating or destroying, love and hate, and the powers of the Universe. They are wonderful.

They are terrible. They are also fallible. Gods are not perfect, but they have greater power over us and yet they take a strong interest in us and our daily lives. It is said that we cannot live without the aid of the gods, but perhaps our relationship with them is more synergistic. As we need the aid of the gods so, too, do the gods need the energy of our prayers, devotions, and ceremonies. However, if we do not worship the gods, does the wind still not blow? If we do not honor the sun, does it still not rise every morning?

Shamans journey to understand the world and the cosmos. When they journeyed to the energy worlds, they may not have understood the energies they were confronted with. Perhaps their mind's eye filtered these energies into human like beings so that they were easier to communicate with. Think about how difficult it would be to have a conversation with a ray of light. I am theorising they had a similar experience with the gods and other spirits, so their mind reshaped the energy into gods that looked like them. This is why the Greek gods look like the Greeks and the Nordic Gods look like the Nordics, etc. This, however, does not make the gods any less real. This is just my theory of how the minds of the shamans saw energies that we now call spirits and gods.

The gods and humans seem to have a synergistic relationship. The gods would provide food (crops, meat, water) for the people and the people would give the gods energy through ceremonials, rituals, and offerings. There are many instances where the people honored the gods to protect their people and land. In Mesopotamia, holy diviners watched the stars for omens to make sure the gods were happy. If not, rituals and sacrifices were made to the gods for their continual protection. In Athens, the Athenians had to honor their patron goddess, Athena, during her holy days to ensure a prosperous city. The brutality of the Aztecs saw the sacrifice of humans to their gods in order to keep the cosmic balance. There was a fear in ancient times that if the gods were not appeased and worshiped in exactly the correct way then the gods would become angry or disinterested in the people and withdraw their power and blessings upon them. I, personally, do not believe that honoring the gods is about doing things exactly right. In my experience and study of the gods, they grant magick and power to people who honor them because it is a reciprocal relationship. For example, if you continually ask your parents for things and never give them anything in return, they will eventually stop helping you. The gods do not need your energies to survive, but they want to be treated with kindness and respect just as you would like to be treated with kindness and respect. Take a moment to think about this for a moment. Have you ever had a friend or relative who was always needing something or seemed to be in trouble all the time? I am sure you helped them gladly. But after a while, did you become frustrated with them never helping you or never giving you anything? That is a one-way relationship. The gods feel the same way. They rarely become angry with us, however they will be disappointed and may withdraw their influence until you begin to pay attention to them again. The gods will always love you, but some lessons are learned without the gods' help.

Worshiping the Gods

Pagans have always loved their gods. Their gods are everything to them and they honor and worship them gladly. They also know that some of the gods are very particular and may become offended easily. Sometimes, we like to think that all the gods are spiritual beings that are constantly enraptured in bliss and understanding. Yes, it is true that the gods are evolved beings with magnificent powers, but they have hopes, desires, and fears just as we do. Some of the gods are very brave and strong, but may lack compassion. Some of the gods are compassionate, but may not understand your human failings. And yet, there are those mysterious gods that control death, fate, and time and care nothing about the trivial squabbles of humans. The gods who we chose to work with and honor can enrich our lives a great deal and teach us how to become better people and more evolved spiritual beings. They can strengthen us and heal us. They have abilities that go beyond space and time.

It is important that we honor the gods to the best of our abilities and with an open heart. There are many pagan teachers who speak of the nature of sacrifice to the gods. Sacrifice does not mean that we kill a living being to give to the gods, but rather, what are we willing to give to a great spirit who is willing to give to us in return? In some modern spiritual communities, it is said God has more than enough to give to everyone. This may be so, but what happens to the child who is constantly taken care of who gives nothing in return? What happens to the integrity of the person whose debts are paid by the divine, but he/ she never has to take responsibility for their actions? When we give offerings or sacrifice to the gods we are doing several things. First, we are entering into a relationship with the gods. We love them and we want to give them something in return. Just as a child gives flowers to their mother or father. Also, it teaches us humility and respect. In the Native American tradition, we always approach the spirits with gratitude. We ALWAYS thank them for the abundance in our lives and each breath that we take each day. We thank them for the sunrise and the lessons of the animal teachers around us. Offerings and sacrifice also has the added benefit of asking ourselves, how much are we willing to give in return for our desires? As humans, we often think we want something very badly, but are not willing to pay the price tag amount. Giving to the gods should always be done out of love and respect and never because it is demanded. We should give to the gods because we want to, never out of obligation. Our gods are our friends and parents, they should always be treated like our family.

Worshiping the gods takes many forms in different parts of the world. There are temples of worship as well as sacred groves. No one way is more holy than another. Each culture does their best to make sure their gods are pleased in which they are honored. There is a temple in Dakshineswar near Kolkata, India, that honors the great Hindu Goddess Kali Ma. Many of the devotees stand for hours in blistering heat to give offerings to the goddess and ask for blessings and healings. As you approach the sacred temple there are many shops where you may purchase red hibiscus flowers and other things as an offering to the deity. It is expected that you are cleansed by the purifying waters of the Ganges River before you go into the temple. The spirit must be cleaned before the goddess gazes upon you. The lines to the main shrine are long and hundreds of people will be scuffling in a line to greet Kali Ma. There is a magnificent statue of the goddess that radiates divine power. The statue is not merely a symbol of the goddess, it IS her. Her divine essence is summoned into the statue and it is treated as if it is the full glory of the goddess herself. Once at the shrine, devotees give the flowers to the priests who place them at Kali Ma's feet. Throughout the day, the flowers will pile up and the priests will have to remove them. Many devotees leave money and incense sticks all in her honor. People may place their hands as close to the statue as they can get and ask for healing and blessings. It is common to hear her sacred chants as tears of joy and devotion roll down the eyes of her loving children.

In Epidaurus, Greece, a temple to Asclepius, the Greek God of Healing, was established around the year 600 BCE. These temples served as a place of worship to the god and a place of healing. Healing temples to Asclepius were established using a holistic approach. They were built around beautiful scenery that gave a sense of comfort. They were also built on or near healing springs. Some of the temple walls were carved with stories of how the god healed the worshiper. This was done in order to begin the process of belief. When a worshiper believed that the god healed others, the healing process was easier for them. The temple priest would instruct the worshiper on the appropriate offerings, usually a cock, and prayers to be given. Then they were given a healing potion that would induce sleep and give dreams. The worshiper was instructed to sleep within the temple of Asclepius in order for the god to heal them. This is referred to as Dream Incubation. Once asleep, the god would appear to them in different forms and take out the sickness and replace it with healing. There are many accounts of Asclepius cutting off someone's head and taking out the malady and insert healing herbs and placing the head back on. Once awake, the priests would interpret the dreams for the worshiper. If someone was too ill to travel to the temple, someone could perform the ritual of dream incubation on their behalf. The temple also served as a place for operations such as removing spear heads from the body, burning and cutting wounds, and amputations of body parts when necessary. Asclepius was one of the most beloved gods of the ancient world and today is known as the "Father of Medicine".

Another form of worship is a *sumbel* that is done during some Heathen ceremonies. A sumbel is the act of "hailing" the gods, ancestors, and other spirits with a drinking horn. Everyone sits or stands in a circle and passes a horn that is full of mead, wine, or ale. Non-alcoholic drinks may be used as well. When the horn comes to each member of the circle they hold the horn high in honor of the gods and make praises to the deity. The horn, itself, is a representation of the Well of Wyrd in Heathen cosmology. *Wyrd* roughly means "Fate". Wyrd is the energy that we put into motion that may define our Fate or Karma later. When we give thanks and hail to the gods we are creating a deeper energetic link. We are weaving our strands of wyrd with those of the gods. The magick of the horn is very powerful and what is said over the horn must come to pass. One may make promises and oaths over the horn, but once this is done it is binding. You are making a verbal contract with the spirits. The sumbel may be done with other spirits as well. Some say that only Heathen spirits should be honored and other say whatever spirit you wish to honor is fine. In my circle, I ask that the first round we honor the spirits we work with then you can honor any god or spirit you like. We can even hail each other and friends who are far away.

The Creator

Olorun Creates the Universe (Ifa)

Olorun is the creator of all things. She is the creator of the Universe and everything that exists in it. Long ago, she wanted to create the heavens and the earth and everything in between. She created a giant magical pot that could contain her magick that would flow down and create all things. But her magick was so powerful that her pot could not contain all of her power. Everytime she tried to create the Universe it would become flooded with hot powerful waters that would destroy everything before it could manifest as creation.

Then one day, Olorun decided that she would create a smaller pot that would hold the overflow of her giant pot and maybe creation would not become flooded and burned. She had a daughter named Olodumare. Olorun gave Olodumare the smaller pot and instructed her on how to catch the overflow of her great big pot. So, Olorun poured her power into her giant pot and when the pot overflowed, Olodumare was able to catch it in her smaller pot and evenly spread out the creative power to create the Universe. To make this so, Olodumare had to create a place in her own magick to allow her mother's magick to cool, in order for creation to manifest. It is through this smaller magical pot of Olodumare that the Orishas (gods) drink and get their magical power and sustenance. This pleased Olorun. She instructed her daughter to allow the Orishas to take the waters and pore it down to earth, each adding a little something of themselves to the water they held. All of creation rejoiced at this wonderfully magick act of manifestation, power, and healing. And so it was. So it is.

In paganism we often call that which created all things "The Creator" or "The Source of All Things". In some Wiccan traditions they call The Creator "The Goddess" the great mother of all things. We rarely say "God" because we believe in many gods and the word "God" is often misunderstood to mean the Judeo-Christian concept of God. In Native American traditions, God is always referred to as the Creator. In African traditions such as Ifa, there is Olorun, who is the Supreme Creator and Deity. She rules the highest heavens and our minds cannot come close to understanding the greatness, which is Olorun. Olorun is actually genderless, but for myth and story sometimes she is referred to as "she" because it is the Mother who creates life. Olorun has a daughter named Olodumare who rules the lower heavens. It is she who gives power to the Orishas so they can rule the heavens and earth. In Kabbalistic traditions, there is the Supreme Deity that is beyond the veils of Ain, Ain Soph, and Ain Soph Aur. Beyond the veils we have the first swirlings of creation we call Keter. This is the highest aspect of God we can understand as humans. This is what we often call the Source, but the

Supreme Deity is beyond even that. If we take a close look at these three cosmologies we see that the Supreme Deity, or Creator, is more or less genderless and is too omnipresent to manifest creation. The Creator must lower its vibration in order to set in motion the energy for creation to manifest. It is after this event, that what we think of as God or Creator, is able to lower its vibration again to create the gods of life, love, war, death, and so on. In the Yoruba (Ifa) tradition, the spiritual energy that is manifested from Olorun to Olodumare to the Orishas, then finally to earth is called *Ashe*. Ashe is what we may call life force, prana, or chi. Ashe come forth from Olorun down to Olodumare then the Orishas then the earth. Everything on earth has Ashe. All things have the essence of Olorun. The gods of Ifa, the Orishas, carry an aspect of Ashe to us here on earth. By examining the cosmology of these traditions, we will better understand how spiritual flows from the Creator down to us.

Choosing a God and Goddess

It is often said in paganism that you do not choose a god or goddess, the gods choose you. In Ifa, it is believed that you have an *ori* or head. Your ori is your God or Goddess that you chose, or they chose you, before your incarnation on this earth. The reason it is called a "head" is because it is believed that your soul/ spirit resides in your head, therefore you personal god would as well. To find out what god or goddess is your personal head, a divination is done by an Ifa priest or priestess. Once your ori is discovered then you must go through an initiation so that your body, mind, and spirit can be aligned to that god.

In modern paganism, most people choose their own personal gods to work with. I personally believe that your personal gods are with you life after life even if you are aware of them or not. Some people believe that your gods are always a part of your cultural lineage. I have found that this is not always true. If you study reincarnation, you will see that we do not always incarnate in the same country over and over again. You may have been a priestess of Apollo in Greece in the year 100 BCE and are a school teacher in New York City today. Once a priestess of Apollo, always a priestess of Apollo. But not everyone shares this same view. Some pagans believe that your personal deities are always your choice, not the will of the gods.

There are some spiritual groups that have their own set of gods and goddesses and if you are initiated into that group then you are expected to honor those gods. In Traditional Witchcraft, once initiated, it is common to do personal offerings and devotions to gods such as Tubal Cain and Frau Holda. In the OTO (Ordo Templi Orientis) the gods are Hadit, Nuit, and Ra-Hoor-Khuit. In Asatru, it is expected that you honor the Asir. The Asir are the Heathen gods that include Odin, Thor, and Freyr. There are countless others, depending on the traditions and belief structure of each group. Normally, you can honor any personal deity you like as long as you honor the deities of the tradition that you are initiated to.

It is not necessary to be initiated into a group to honor the gods. An initiation, more or less, aligns your energies to a specific current of energy. It may be a deity or it may be the magical current of that specific group. One of the best and easiest ways to find your personal gods is through research, prayer, and meditation. What mythologies and pagan pantheons are you attracted to? Are you attracted to the Greek Pantheon or Egyptian? Or is it Native American? Or perhaps it's Heathen. Race does not matter. I know many people who are attracted to Vodou and Ifa who are Latino or Caucasian. I also know African Americans who are drawn to Celtic and Heathen traditions. A word of advice, any group that does not allow you in because of your race or sexual preference is not a group you want to be in. Once you find a couple of pantheons you are attracted to, you need to read the myths. Take your time and enjoy the stories. Which ones resonate with you? Which god and goddess do you feel a kindred spirit with? In her book *Kali: The Black Goddess of Dakshineswar,* Elizabeth U. Harding says, "There must be some similarity between the adorer and the adored. For instance, a worshiper of Kali has some attributes of Kali in him or her, and likewise, a worshiper of Shiva has Shiva attributes. Otherwise he or she wouldn't feel attracted to that particular deity." If you are a healer (massage therapist, energy worker, doctor, nurse) pay special attention to the myths of healer deities. If you are in computers, education, and writing, pay attention to deities that govern communication and logic. Once you find a god and goddess you like, journey to their home or temple and speak with them. Ask them if they are your patron deities. If they are not, ask them to direct you to the deities who are. When you meet your patron gods, it should feel like a homecoming. Like you are seeing a long lost parent or friend.

Ceremony To Discover Your Personal Gods

You will need a white candle and incense that takes your mind and spirit to the world of the gods. You can pick anything you like, but for this ceremony, I prefer something like sage, frankincense, sandalwood or rosemary.

1. State your intention to meet and discover your gods

2. Light your candle and incense and meditate on spirit, the gods, and your wish to connect with deity.

3. Journey to the Upperworld and speak with your Upperworld Guide. Tell him/her of your desire to meet your gods and ask

them to take you to them.

4. Allow the journey to unfold naturally.

5. When you meet the gods ask them if they are your patron and matron. You may only meet one of your gods. That is Ok. If the deities you meet are not your gods, ask them to take you to the one who are.

6. When you meet your gods ask them their names and how they would like to be honored.

7. If you do not meet your gods on this journey, then upon returning to waking consciousness, ask your gods to reveal themselves to you very soon.

8. Record your journey and outcome in your journal.

Creating A God Altar

Creating a sacred shrine for your gods is one of the most fun and fulfilling things we can do as a pagan. After you have discovered who your patron and matron gods are you will want to find a statue in their likeness. Pantheons such as Greco-Roman, Heathen, and Egyptian are probably the easiest. Many online stores and shops have them. If you cannot find the exact statue you are looking for, you can improvise. I have seen many beautiful female statues that made a great statue for Isis, Venus, Mother Earth and so forth. In some traditions such as Traditional Witchcraft, you do not necessarily use a statue for the god, you use a stang or a goat skull. Other traditions may use wooden objects or cauldrons full of herbs, stones, and sticks. For our purposes here, we will focus on the statuary. If you are initiated to a specific tradition ask your teachers and initiators what is traditional for your group.

When you have obtained your statutes, it is common to place your gods in the back of the altar; the goddess to the left and the god to the right. This has more to do with a Kabbalistic correspondence of the female pillar of the Tree of Life is to the left and the male pillar is to the right. Feel free to do whatever is suited to your taste. The gods may even tell you where they prefer their statues. Each god will need their own candle, which is to be lit each time you speak with them or give them devotions. You will then want to place incense somewhere on the altar. You can place it in the center of the altar, the east (for air), or in the very front. It is really up to you. I personally, place offering bowls before each of the god statues. You can remove them when not doing offerings, but I like to keep them on the altar. If you so choose, you can place any magical tools, talismans, crystals, or magical jewelry. You can also add decorations if you like. You may place seasonal decor such as pumpkins for Samhain, candles for Imbolc, flowers for Beltane, and wheat for Lughnasadh. I like to put things that resonate with me and my gods.

Devotion - Bhakti

Having a relationship with the divine is one of the most important aspects of Universal existence. In Hinduism, there is the spiritual practice of *Bhakti*. Bhakti means "the intense love of God". There are many forms of Bhakti. There is *santa* which is the peaceful love of the gods. This means that we have a general love of the gods but do not feel the intense passion to love. This is considered the lowest form of Bhakti. Then there is *dasya*, the servitude of the gods. This is being of service to the gods, but in dasya there is no intense love. There is also *sakhya*, this is being a friend to the gods. In this relationship, we treat the gods as a best friend and companion. The energy exchange here is more or less equal and one is not higher nor more sacred than the other. *Vatsalya* is the form of Bhakti that our relationship with the gods is that they are our children. We love them and take care of them as if they are our own children. In this relationship, there is no fear of the gods and we nurture the divine. Then there is the opposite of this where the gods are our parents and our caretakers.

In Bhakti, the highest form of love for the gods is called *madhura*. This is an intense passionate romantic love for the gods. This is the kind of love to where one is literally in love with their god and goddess. We can find examples of this type of love all through mythology. The first that comes to mind is Psyche and Eros. Eros, the god of erotic love fell in love with the mortal, Psyche and would only visit her at night. When she confronted him in the dark, he flew away only to be reunited with her after many days of divine testing. In some Luciferian traditions it is believed that Lucifer refused to bow before man because of his intense romantic love of God. He felt betrayed by his beloved so his battle and exile from heaven was that of a lover scorned. But because of his love for God, he spends his days trying to help humans spiritually evolve so that, after they are returned to heaven, he may be redeemed and return to his beloved.

Swami Vivekananda says in his book *Karma-Yoga and Bhakti-Yoga*, "All loves and all passions of the human heart must go to God. He is the beloved. Whom else can this heart love? He is the most beautiful, the most sublime; he is beauty itself, sublimity itself. Who in this universe is more beautiful than he? Who in this universe is more fit to become the husband than He? Who in this universe is more fit to be loved than He? So let Him be the husband; let him be the Beloved."

Your relationship with the gods may change over time. At times you may see them as a parent and at others, a friend, and still at others, a lover. I, personally, view my patron god and goddess as parents. I feel that they take care of my wants and needs and in return, I give them respect, devotions, and love. I think that it is up to each of us to decide how our relationship with the gods should be. One word of caution, if you decide to have a romantic relationship exclusively with the gods they may become jealous with your mortal relationships. There have been many tales of how a marriage "mysteriously" broke up once an initiate was magically married to their patron god or goddess. In Vodou, the lwa (spirit) Ezili Freda will grant her followers with sexual prowess, love, luck, and wealth, but she is very jealous. It is taboo to have sex near her shrine and it is said if her shrine is in the bedroom she may become jealous of your lovers and break up your relationship.

Meditation

Once you have discovered your god and goddess you will need to spend time with them. Light your god altar and light incense that is pleasing to them. Meditate with them. You can journey to them if you like, but it is not necessary. Remember, the gods can be in multiple places at once and space and time have no meaning for them. They can enter your heart and consciousness at any time. If you would like, create a sacred space for them in the astral plane by simply visualizing a garden, a temple, or grove that is pleasing to both you and the gods. Visit them in this astral sacred space and get to know the gods.

Offerings and Sacrifice

In pagan tradition it is taught to give offerings and sacrifice to the gods. It is better if you research what was once given to your god and goddess. There are also taboos that you want to honor. For example, some gods do not like raw meat and to offer sushi or raw beef is considered impolite. Other gods, such as Asclepius, love when an offering of a cockerel is given to them. In modern times, most neo-pagans do not give a sacrifice of a live animal, so a cooked cockerel or hen is very acceptable. That being said, in some Vodou traditions it is very acceptable to give the sacrifice of live animals. It may sound horrible to our Western sensibilities but think of it this way; up until a hundred years ago when you wanted chicken for dinner you went to your chicken coop and slaughtered a live chicken and cooked it. The only difference is that you gave the blood to the gods. The rule of thumb I go by is that I try my best to research what they like and dislike, as well as simply ask them during meditation. The gods have indeed been exposed to modern day culture. Some gods may prefer a chocolate bar to a bowl of milk. But, they may want both!

Petition Magick

Petition magick is one of the oldest forms of magick. This form of magick is done by writing down your request on parchment or paper and giving it to the gods. It can be placed on the god altar or it can be burned. A very simple form of petition magick is to simply light the candles on your god altar, light the incense, and simply ask your gods to grant your request.

Ritual of Devotion To The God and Goddess

It is important to give devotions to your gods on a weekly basis. When we give devotions, it strengthens the energetic link with our gods. This link is very important because it will allow you to spiritually progress on your path much faster. Also, the gods will be willing to help you more than if you did not. We all have known people who ask us for help but never return the favor. Most of us, being good people, will help if needed, but we may do it reluctantly. However, our friends who spend time with us we are willing to help gladly. This is the same for the gods. Yes, the gods have the power to help us, but if we do not give them energy as they give us energy their link with us will be weak and their blessings may be limited.

Items needed: God Altar set up

Offerings of incense, food, flowers and/or wine

Bowl of water

1. Purification

    When we begin, we will want to ritually clean ourselves and our space. We can do an energetic wipe down, smudge, fumigate, or use a besom. An easy way to purify, is to see a bright ball of light coming from our solar plexus. See this ball expand over our body, purifying us, then expanding to our temple space, purifying every-thing within.

2. Ritual intent

    Say out loud your intent. Use your own words but you can say something like, "I have come today to honor the gods."

3. Center, Ground, Shield and Connect to Three Worlds.

    Center, ground, and shield yourself energetically. Also, connect to the three worlds. You can use the neo-pagan tree meditation or simply allow your energies to connect to the three worlds. The neo-pagan tree meditation: As you exhale, send tendrils of your energy down to the core of the earth through your feet. If sitting, through your tailbone. On the inhale, breath in the fires of the center of the earth in your belly. Do this three times. Focus on your crown. As you exhale, send tendrils of energy from your head to the center of the universe above. On the inhale, bring in celestial energy down into your heart. Allow the energies of earth and sky to mix.

4. Meditate on God and Goddess

Light the god and goddess candles. Bring to mind your god and goddess. If you only know of one, you may simply focus on one. Think of their attributes and characteristics. You may read their myths or poems if you like.

5. Evoke Gods in Your Heart.

In your heart, summon the images of your gods. Feel their presents in your heart and feel your love for them. Allow this love to give them energy and vitality. You may chant their names or read a poem or myth. Feel an intense desire for them to manifest.

6. Manifest the Gods into Statue

To manifest the gods. Focus on the gods in your heart, have an intense desire for them to manifest. Take a deep breath and on the exhale breath the spirit of the gods from your heart into the statues. At this time, you can continue to send them love or you can chant their names again or read another poem in their honor.

7. Offerings

At this time, give offerings of incense, food, flowers, and/or wine. When you have developed your clairvoyant skills, you will see the statues radiate with power and gratitude. If you have a limited budget, it is ok just to give offerings of incense and water. The gods care more about your intent and love then extravagant offerings. However, the more you sacrifice for your gods the more blessings you will receive.

8. Journey to the Astral Temple of the Gods

The gods are not restricted to our three dimensional world. They are in many places at once. We can show more devotion and have a deeper understanding of them if we journey to them in their temple. If you have Upperworld gods you will go to the Upperworld, if Underworld gods then Underworld, if Midworld gods then Midworld.

Astral project to the sacred place of your gods. Spend some time talking with them and giving them love. You can ask them for advice on matters or ask them for magick or a blessing. Return to your body when you are ready.

9. Energy Exchange

When you are back in your body. See the god statues radiating with power. Feel the full presence of your gods. As you exhale, give energy to them gods from your heart. The gods will give you energy in return. Breathe this energy into your heart. Allow this sacred exchange of energy to remain for a few moments.

10. Water Blessing

Using the bowl of water on the altar, see the gods fill the water with energy, blessings, and healing. Take the water bowl and sprinkle some water over your head and body. Bless your temple space with it, then drink the rest.

11. Divination

At this time, you may do a divination if you chose. You can use tarot, runes, geomancy, or any other oracle. I usually ask to see my upcoming future and any advice on handling any situations I am currently dealing with.

12. End Ceremony

State that the ceremony has ended. If you like allow the god candles to burn for a while and allow the incense to burn out, otherwise, you can blow out the candles and put out the incense. Feel the energy dissipate back into the astral/ spiritual plane.

Evocation

The act of evocation means to call the gods and spirits into your magical space. The difference between evocation and invocation is that *invocation* calls the gods and spirits into your body for magical and ritual purposes. The gods that we honor and work with in our lives have an active interest in us. They want to help us succeed our our spiritual path and our daily lives. We evoke deities into our magical space for many reasons.

1. Devotion

2. Magical protection during ritual

3. Guidance and wisdom

4. Blessings and healing

5. Spellcraft

It is relatively simple to evoke a deity into your magical space. If you have meditated with your gods and performed devotions all you have to do is simply tune into them energetically and call to them. If you have established an energetic link to the gods all you have to do is ask them to manifest in your space. Remember, the gods are not our servants and they are not mandated to appear in your ritual or magical operation. To have a god bless your space or aide you in magick truly a gift and they should be given offerings and thanks to show your gratitude.

Invocation

Invocation means to call a deity or spirit in your body for magick or ritual purposes. The magical act of invocation has been used by the Egyptians to call Osiris into the Pharaoh, by the Greeks to call Apollo in the Oracle of Delphi, by Neo-Pagans to call the Goddess into the High Priestess, and animal spirits into shamans. This divine act of magick is used to further the relationship with worshipers and their gods. It is one of the most personal and powerful ways to establish a direct connection with the gods. In this way, there is no need for an interpreter of the message of the gods. You are having an intimate experience with the divine.

With training, anyone can invoke a god into their body. Just as with anything, there are some people who have a talent for this skill and others who must continue to practice. Divine experience of all types is open to anyone who is willing to open their heart to the gods. The important things to remember about invocation is that you must establish a personal relationship to the god you are invoking and you must have spiritual discipline. What I mean by discipline is that you must learn the basics of energy control, deity mythology and cultural context, centering and grounding, and self awareness. Self awareness is probably the most difficult. To be effective as magical practitioners, we must understand our strengths and weaknesses as well as our hopes, fears, desires, and prejudices.

When we invoke a god or goddess we will be taking their personality into our bodies. We will also be taking in their strengths and weaknesses. My patron deity is Asclepius, the God of Healing. When I invoke him, his energy heals my body, mind, and spirit. I have studied his mythologies, gave him devotions, and meditated with him. I am aware of his powers and abilities and welcome them into my personal rituals and healings. However, when I invoke Diana, my matron goddess, she is quite different. Yes, she has the power to heal, but she is the goddess of the moon, the hunt, and outcasts of society. She is fierce and an unmarried (virgin) goddess. When she controls my body for ritual she expects my body to be healthy and my life to be disciplined. Personally, I strive to have a balance between work, magick, and relationships. From my experience with Diana, nothing is more important than magick and helping the less fortunate. When I invoke Diana regularly, her personality will begin to influence mine if I do not have self-awareness. It was said in ancient Greece and Rome that it is unwise to invoke Hades/Pluto because by doing so is to invite death into your temple space. If you have read my previous book *Underworld: Shamanism, Myth, and Magick* then you know that I have no issues with inviting death into my ritual space.

I feel that invoking your personal god and goddess will strengthen your relationship with them and help you upon your magical journey. Your love for them will grow and so will the bond between them and you. That being said, I would like to caution you on a few things. Do not invoke any god you are not aware of and have not read their mythologies. You do not want a god in your body that contrasts your values and ethics. You do not want to invoke the trickster god, Loki, for a ritual for justice. You may get justice, but not according to your ideals, but rather justice from the point of you of the trickster. It may not go according to plan. You also do not want to invoke an Egyptian deity to a Native American healing ceremony. Many gods from around the world are called upon for healing, but and Egyptian deity will not be familiar with Native American tribal ceremonies and it shows that deity that you do not know how to properly honor the god that you have invoked.

Being in a good condition of physical, mental, and emotional health is something to consider. It takes a lot of energy to invoke a god and if you are sick or run down then it may make your condition worse. Also, many ancient pagan cultures believed that to honor the body was to honor the gods. The Greek Olympics was established to honor the gods through physical skill. The Nordic warriors believed that one honored

Odin by giving everything they had on the battlefield, including their lives if necessary. Native American hunters believed that having skill in the hunt honored the people as well as the Creator. That being said, you do not have to be in perfect health and strength to invoke the gods. The gods ask that you do your best and they will be honored.

Do not be worried about being possessed by demons or spirits who are not your god or goddess. The only time a lesser spirit is able to possess a person is if they allow it or they are mentally and physically unstable. If your aura is strong it acts as a powerful psychic protective shield that will not allow anything in unless you allow it. Also, when you have been working with your god and goddess, you have established a bond with them and they will not allow another spirit to join with your body. I am a child of Diana, and one does not cross the goddess of the moon. There are many myths of those who offended her and did not do well because of it. People who suffer from drug or alcohol addiction have a more difficult time keeping their auras strong. This is one of the reasons why it is not wise to be drunk when doing invocation. However, it is OK if, while invoked, the god drinks alcohol. YOU are not drinking it, the god is.

It is a good idea to have a magically experienced teacher, friend, or colleague to help you when you invoke for the first couple of times. This way, you will feel a bit safer and can go deeper in your invocation. Also, if something were to happen, which is very rare, your friend can help you un-invoke and ground the energy and do any healing if need be.

Types of Invocation

There are several different types of invocation. Just as any magical practice, there are levels for the novice as well as levels for advanced practitioners. One is not more sacred than another, but rather a deeper level of commitment and magical training. I am presenting the different types of invocation that I was taught. Each tradition may teach invocation differently and may have many more levels that I am presenting here, but here are the basics to get you started.

Play Acting

This is not traditionally considered invocation, but more akin to acting as if you were performing in a play. This form of invocation usually has a set dialogue or lines that the god or goddess gives. I have seen this form in many rituals. Usually, this is good for those practitioners who are beginners to invocation. I do not think this is inferior than the other forms of invocation. I have seen many rituals that do a lovely job of teaching the congregation of the deity's mythology and stories. There is usually no actual god energy that the ritualist invokes.

Aspecting

This is a form of invocation that brings some of the god's energy into the body of the ritualist but they still remain in control. The amount of control the ritualist gives the deity depends upon their experience and energy control as well as the purpose of the ritual in question. For example, I have the ability to allow for full possession from a god, but if I am performing a ritual I may need some control to keep the flow of the ritual going according to plan. Some gods have a tendency to do what they want in ritual and not what you want. Aspecting is also good for ritualist who have not developed full trust in invocation and may feel more comfortable with only allowing a god a certain percentage of control over their body. Usually, the god remains mostly in control but the ritualist is aware of what is happening and can take control of their body at any time. From my experience, this feels like I am sharing my body with deity.

Possession

Possession is when the deity has full control of the ritualist's body. When this happens the god takes over the body and the ritualist has very little, if any control. In ritual, you are in the full presence of a god. You can feel the energy of the divine coming from their aura and the eyes of a god are looking upon you. Sometimes, this allows for a greater degree of magick and "miracles" to occur. In Vodou and Ifa rituals, you can see full possession all the time. Possession is a part of the ritual structure and many people, who attend these rituals and honor the Vodou gods, are very aware that anyone can become possessed at anytime. It is considered a blessing from the gods to be chose to "horse" a god. In order to do this, the ritualist must open up their energies to allow the god to enter their body and consciousness. This takes a great deal of trust in the god to do this. The best way to learn possession is to establish a deep connection with the gods through meditation, honoring, and devotion to the gods.

Invocation Technique for Aspecting and Possession

Spend at least a week or so doing devotions and meditating with your patron god. Pay attention to their energies and the wisdom and insight they give you.

1. Center, ground, and shield. Light your god candle and incense as an offering.

2. Close your eyes. Allow your heart chakra to open and have the very strong desire to have union with your god.

3. With an intense desire from your heart, call upon your god to appear behind you.

4. See your god the best you can. Visualize their face, body, cloths, and any tools or armor. Tune in to their energies.

5. Again, feel the intense desire to join with your god. Feel energy from your god's heart chakra blend into your heart chakra from behind. Your heart energies become one.

6. Visualize the god step into your body as if they were putting on clothes. See them step into your legs and feet as if they were pants. See them put their hands and arms into your hands and arms as if they were putting on sleeves.

7. Visualize them join their torso to your torso and their head to your head. Feel god's heart join your heart to become one heart.

8. See the god join their head with your head, their mind with your mind, their eyes with your eyes.

9. Take a few breaths and allow the god to merge with your consciousness and your body.

10. The god has control over your body. As the god opens their eyes your eyes are open.

11. You can go as deep as you feel comfortable. If you want to allow full possession, allow the god's consciousness to go to the forefront of your mind while your consciousness is put to the side.

To Un-Invoke a God or Goddess

To release a god from your body, the technique is more or less reversed.

1. Allow your consciousness to become more dominant in your body.

2. Feel the god disconnect from your mind. Feel them let go of your

eyes, mouth, and ears.

3. Feel the union of your hearts disengage and feel the separation of your heart and your god's heart.

4. Visualize your god taking off your arms and torso as if taking off a shirt.

5. Visualize your god taking their legs out of your legs as if taking off pants.

6. Feel your god completely disengage from your heart.

7. Visualize your god behind you. Give thanks and gratitude for their aide in your magick. See them disappear into the astral plane.

8. Give offerings to your gods.

5
Angels

In the Judeo-Christian cosmology there are higher spiritual beings we call angels. The world "angel" comes from the Greek word *angelos* meaning "messenger". Angels are described as beings of light and fire when they are not taking human shape. In our modern day, angels are typically thought of as higher helping spirits who guide mankind. They are sometimes seen as divine healers. They certainly can be these things but when we work with angels shamanistically and magically, we find that they are more complex than what we think of as guardian angels.

Their role in the Universe is to make sure everything is running smoothly in accordance to the will of God.

I am sometimes asked by students, "If we are working with a neo-pagan shamanistic path, why do we work with angels?" The Upperworld is full of advanced spiritual beings and angels are one of the many entities that we work with. When it comes down to it, it does not matter where the magick comes from as long as we get the results we desire. Traditional witches are infamous for learning magical secrets from whomever they came in contact with. They were not so much concerned with who the magick came from but rather did it work? Angels can be extremely helpful and are one of the most powerful entities in the Upperworld.

If we study texts such as *Book of Enoch* and *The Old Testament* we can see that angels have the power to keep the universe running according to the divine plan. They are responsible for many things such as the revolution of the planets around the sun, time, the placement of stars and constellations, magick, divination, the powers of the oceans, winds, and growing things on the earth, as well as many other things. When we look at shamanism, we see that everything has an indwelling spirit that controls the growth of plants and trees, the powers of the sun and moon, the rocks, the winds, fire, and everything else in the

Universe. In tribal cultures, such as the Native Americans, all energies are personified. All energies from rainstorms to the rising and setting of the sun have energies that people did not understand. To better help understand these energies, ancient peoples personified the energies and gave the personalities that fit their natural characteristics. When patriarchal religions came into being, they believed that any spirit, other than angels or god himself, that were associated with power had to be demonic. Therefore, Judeo-Christian religion simply gave the duties of the tribal spirits to the angels.

I originally learned to work with angels through ceremonial magick, but I have learned, over time, that you do not need to call them through long invocations chanted from ancient texts. Although, I still enjoy a traditional grimoire from time to time. I personally work with them in a few ways. I ask for their protection and guidance when I work with spirits that vibrate on a lower plane such as Goetic demons. One of the simplest ways to evoke them is through the Lesser Banishing Ritual of the Pentagram. There is a section of that ritual where you simply intone the names of the Archangels. I also journey to them whenever I need to ask them to teach me some of their expertise. One example is time travel. Angels have the ability to travel through time and space and predict the future.

Angels also have the power to heal. The Archangel Raphael is known as the angelic healer. Recently, new agers have been criticized for being too "white light" when it comes to working with angels. Angels are sometimes described as terrifying yet beautiful and are concerned with the powers of the Universe versus day-to-day human affairs. I have worked with many healing spirits and I can see why some healers call these beings angels. Those who come from a Judeo-Christian background are unaware of the many spirits that help us heal through energy work.

I myself work with the Greek Healing god Asclepius, Reiki Ascended Masters, My Native American ancestors, and several others. Some healers perceive these energies as beings of light. To them, it makes perfect sense that these would be angels. Perhaps they are angels, perhaps not. There are millions of angels in the Universe and I believe that some of them do take an interest in humanity and help us heal and spiritually advance.

There is a lot of information about Angelic Magick from medieval grimoires that are readily available to us. I particularly enjoy the books, such as *The Key of Solomon The King* by S.L. MacGregor Mathers, that teach us how to summon angels and evoke their magick for spells and talismans. I have also seen grimoires that teach how to bind an angel to do your will. The path of the shaman honors all spirits and has respect for them. My very first teacher, Matthew Ellenwood, taught me that we should always have a working relationship with spirits. We never treat spirits poorly and force them to do anything.

Angels are very powerful beings and can do very powerful things. They can teach us the ways of the Universe and of magick. They can empower our rituals to bring us wonderful results. They can also guide us through aspects of our higher consciousness and spiritual evolution. To have angels as allies will be very helpful upon your path as a shaman, witch, or magician.

The Four Archangels

Archangels are the "higher" angels that lead or rule a type of lesser angels. These angels can be described as grand architects that help build the Universe according to the divine plan of God. The Four archangels who govern the elements are not the same as the archangels who govern the sephiroths of Yesod, Hod, Netzach, and Tiphereth, and so forth.

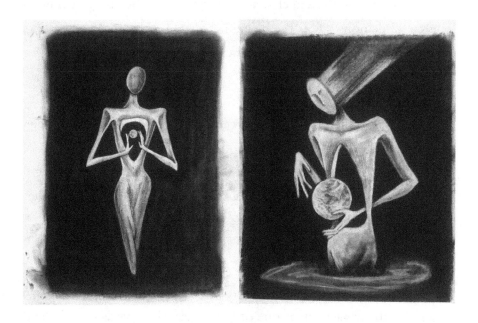

Some Kabbalists believe that they are archangels who reside only in Malkuth, the physical plane. Perhaps this is so, but these are the four archangels of the physical universe as we know it.

If we remember the section of this book that speaks of the Big Bang and the energies that came out of it. We have gravity that can be seen as fire. Electromagnetic force that can be seen as air. Strong nuclear force that can be seen as earth and weak nuclear force that can be seen as water . It is interesting to speculate that perhaps these four archangels were created as a result of the Big Bang or maybe God assigned the four archangels the task of bringing these forces into our physical universe.

Raphael

Governs the element of air. He wears yellow robes highlighted in violet and holds the caduceus. He is considered the "friendliest" of the archangels. He is the angel that gave Solomon the magical ring to command demons. He is the divine healer. He is the angle of healing, science, and music. He also rules the Sun.

Michael

Governs the element of fire. He wears red robes highlighted in green and holds a flaming sword. He is considered the greatest of all angels, some others say this title belongs to Metatron. He is credited with defeating Satan. He is the divine warrior. He is the angel of mercy, justice, and repentance. He also rules the planet of Mercury.

Gabriel

Governs the element of water. He wears blue robes highlighted in orange and holds the chalice. He is one of the angels who guards paradise and animated the Golden Calf. In Biblical lore, he is the angel that sounds the great horn that brings the apocalypse. Angel of resurrection, truth, and vengeance. He also rules the planet of the Moon.

Ariel/Uriel

Governs the element of earth. He wears green robes highlighted in brown and holds the pentacle. The names Ariel and Uriel are sometimes interchangeable. Has the power to control demons and rules over Hell. He is credited to giving the Kabbalah and alchemy to mankind. He also aides Raphael with healing.

Angelic Magick
Evocation of the Four Archangels

In many neo-pagan and ceremonial traditions, the four archangels are called into the temple, or magical space, for protection, guidance, and magick. There are many techniques and ceremonies in which the archangels are called. I have a very simple and effective ritual you can do in your daily practice that will help you connect with the archangels and they will also add psychic protection for your throughout the day. When speaking the angelic name, be sure to intone or sing the name in bold letters.

1. Stand facing East. Center and ground yourself. Calm your breath and turn within.

2. Connect with the cosmic web of the Universe and connect with the fabric of all existence.

3. Bring your attention to the east and say, "I call to the great Archangel **Raphael**, Keeper of the Gate of the East." Visualize Raphael with Yellow robes, highlighted in purple. There is the element of Air all around him and he holds the caduceus staff.

4. Bring your attention to the south and say, "I call to the great archangel **Michael**, Keeper of the Gate of the South." Visualize Michael wearing red robes, highlighted in green. There is the element of Fire all around him and he holds the flaming sword.

5. Bring your attention to the west and say, "I call the to the great archangel **Gabriel**, Keeper of the Gate of the West." Visualize Gabriel wearing blue robes, highlighted in orange. There is the element of Water all around him and he holds the chalice.

6. Bring your attention to the north and say, " I call to the great archangel **Ariel**, Keeper of the Gate of the North." Visualize Ariel wearing green robes, highlighted in brown. There is the element of earth all around him and he holds the pentacle.

7. Feel the presence of the four arch angels around you. Feel how they are protecting and guiding you. Then say, "Great archangels, I ask that you protect me this day and offer guidance upon my sacred path of spirit."

8. Allow the archangels to disappear from your sight and know that they are still there even though you cannot see them.

Speaking with the Archangels

The archangels not only can offer you protection and guidance but they can also offer you great wisdom. They are the governors of the great magick that pertains to their element. They are wonderful teachers and can show you many amazing things. You can speak with the angels directly and ask them questions and ask for advice, wisdom, and magick. To do this, simply perform the above evocation technique. This time you are going to add the following:

1. Light four candles, one in each of the four directions. Yellow for

east, red for south, blue for west, and green for north.

2. Perform the above evocation.

3. Choose an archangel that can best offer you wisdom or advice in accordance to their nature. East-communications, travel, mind; South-energy, passion, creativity; West-emotions, relationships, intuition; Earth-health, jobs, home.

4. Once an archangel is chosen, stand facing them in the appropriate direction. Ask them the question you have or you may ask them to teach you the magick of their element. They may speak plainly or may send you symbols or thoughts to your mind. You can also ask them to come to your dreams.

5. When ready thank the angels for their assistance. See the angels fade from your sight and blow out the candles.

Watchers/ Grigori

The Watchers are the angels that lusted after the daughters of men and fell from heaven. Sometimes the angels that watch over the human race are referred to as the "Watchers". They are not the "demonic" or fallen angels of the Bible who were thrown out of heaven for fighting against God in the Great War. Some of the Watchers chose to fall from their position so that they may walk upon the earth and have sex with women and sometimes men. Those who "fell" are also sometimes called the Grigori. I have found in some Traditional Witchcraft circles The Watchers, The Grigori, and the Niflheim are all used interchangeably.

In myth, it is sometimes said that the reason that the Watchers fell is because of a Promethean philosophy. As the angels watched mankind, they grew concerned that the new creatures of God had no technology. They had no fire, no tools, no knowledge of herbal medicine and the magick of the stars. A group of Watchers then fell in lust or love with the women on earth and decided to be with them and teach them the ways of magick, healing, and tool making. In Judeo-Christian myth, when we say that one third of the angels "fell" from heaven, what they mean is that they were forcibly removed and that they fell from their spiritual position in their divine order of the Universe. When we speak of the Grigori falling, what we mean is that they gave up their celestial authority, as given to them by God, and "fell" from spirit into the world of matter. In the magical circles I belong to, we call upon the Watchers and the Nephilim to teach us the magick of stars, star portals, healing, and other magicks.

Here are some of the Watchers that taught magick to mankind.

Azazel taught smith crafting. How to make tools and weapons. He also taught how to beautify oneself with makeup. He taught the crafting and magical use of precious and semi-precious stones. He is sometimes associated with the Witch god, Tubal Cain.

Semjaza taught how to cast spells and the magick of roots.

Armaros taught how to defend oneself against magical spells.

Baraqijal taught astrology.

Kokabel taught the constellations, stars, and their magick.

Ezeqeel taught about significance of clouds and what they mean.

Araquiel taught about the signs and omens of the earth and its inhabitants.

Shamsiel taught about the signs of the sun.

Sariel taught about the movement of the moon.

Summoning The Grigori

In Traditional Witchcraft, we sometimes call upon the Grigori/ Watchers to our ritual space for use in guidance and magick. In my own personal experience with them, they work a little differently than other angelic beings such as archangels or their legion of angels. Most angels have a very light-divine energy, where the Grigori do have an angelic presence but they have a more earthy or shadowed feel. Do not confuse them with demons. They are not demonic, even though they did go against the word of God. As we have seen in the myths, these angels are more closely connected with the earth and human affairs; whereas, other angels are more concerned with the divine order of the Universe.

How I have summoned them in my circle is to call them by name and ask for their presence in the ritual space. You can also journey to them by asking the aid of your Upperworld guide. They are great teachers of magick, astrology and many other things.

Nephilim

The Nephilim, meaning *fallen,* are the offspring of the fallen angels and human women. In the *Book of Enoch,* they are considered demons that are abominations against the creation of God. They are said to have devoured all the food and cattle of humanity and once they were done with that they began to eat human flesh and populate the earth. In some stories, the fallen Watchers only had sex with the children of Cain and bred an evil race of "men". This evil race turned away from God and needed to be purged from the earth with a great flood. In some forms of angel magick in Traditional Craft, The Watchers and Nephilim are sometimes interchangeable and we will often call the angelic Nephilim to help us with celestial magick and technology. It is interesting to note that the Lord or Master of the Witches of Traditional Craft is Tubal Cain, the first blacksmith. This technology would have been taught to him by the Watchers/ Nephilim. In some Traditional Witchcraft circles Tubal Cain and Azazel, the angel of blacksmithing, are one and the same; they simply take on a different form depending upon the role they play. I personally have experienced them to be distinct and separate entities.

The Watchers and Nephilim can be very helpful in magick. They can teach you the skills and disciplines of magick. There are a few different ways you can easily work with then. You can journey to speak with them or you can evoke them in your temple space. You can also have them empower ritual objects such as charms and spells.

Enoch

Enoch, the son of Jared, walked the earth around the time of Noah in the Old Testament. The children of the fallen Watchers had become very powerful and wicked according to Jewish belief structure. They were a disease upon the earth that needed to become cleansed. God was planning a great flood that would clean the earth from the Niflheim. Enoch was very special to God. In his book *The Book of Enoch: The Angels, The Watchers, and the Nephilim,* Joseph B. Lumpkin says God chose Enoch to walk with him because he is "…as the best mankind has to offer and God took him as an act of admiration, indicating the intended worth of mankind, had they had not turned away from him."

Enoch's Ascent (Judaism)

Enoch was a man of God. Even when those around him were selfish and unkind, it was he who kept his faith in the Creator God above. The world has grown dark with the evil deeds of men. God, the creator, was going to wash away the evil of the earth and begin again with Noah. But God had taken notices of Enoch. It was he who would be the intercessory between the worlds of men and the heavens with its angels. One day, Enoch was approached by two angels and was taken to heaven.

Enoch knew he was about to have a great adventure, but the journey would not only be incredible but frightening as well.

During his ascent to the throne of God he saw that there were ten heavens.

On their arrival of The First Heaven he saw

Storehouses of snow and dew that would fall upon the earth.

On their arrival to the Second Heaven he saw

The Fallen angels, those who fought the battle in heaven against God

In this Heaven there was only Darkness and Torture

On their arrival to the Third Heaven he saw

That this was a place of Sweet flowers, trees, and fruit

On their arrival to the Fourth Heaven he saw

Then Angelic Soldiers, heaven's army, and the progression of the sun and moon.

On their arrival to the Fifth Heaven he saw

The leaders of the Grigori, the fallen angels who went down to earth and had sex with the daughters of men.

On their arrival to the Sixth Heaven He saw

seven bands of angels and the ordering of stars and constellations

On their arrival to the Seventh Heaven he saw

That something unusual was happening

when Enoch was at the throne of God.

On their arrival to the Eighth Heaven he saw

The Zodiac And the magick it possessed

On their arrival to the Ninth Heaven he saw

The Heavenly bodies themselves, which were the stars

On their arrival to the Tenth Heaven he saw

That God's face is revealed

Then Enoch began to change, His face glowed like fire embers and his eyes cast out sparks of light and fire.

It is here that Enoch is transformed into an angel named Metatron

And it is before the face of God that Enoch's flesh is "shed" and he is transformed into an angel. The Book of Enoch says, "This Enoch, whose flesh is turned into flame, his veins to fire, his eyelashes flashes of lightning, his eyes flaming torches."

He is transformed into the Angel Metatron, who sits just beneath the throne of God. He is taught by the angels about all things in heaven and earth. He is taught about the celestial bodies and the stars and the universe.

Exercise: Journeying to Meet Metatron

Metatron is the angel that is closest to the throne of God/ Creator. As far as we know from The Bible, no other mortal person has ever been transformed into an angel. However, there have been some who have ascended to heaven, but they are not angels. Metatron is also unique because he was once human so, therefore, he retains a human perspective that the other angels do not have. Off all the archangels, he understands our human frailties, weaknesses, faults, etc. He is the most powerful and yet the most understanding. Metatron is a being that can help you greatly upon your path of spiritual evolution.

1. Get comfortable, close your eyes, and place yourself in a trance state. You may burn a single white candle and incense correspond-ing with Keter.

2. Focus on the physical plane. Take a few deep breaths and allow your mind to focus on the astral counterpart of the physical plane, Malkuth. Take a moment and notice the transition of color, feeling, and sensation of Malkuth.

3. Visualize yourself going up the Kabbalistic Tree of Life. See yourself upon the path leading from Malkuth to Yesod. Yesod is the Kabbalistic sphere of Foundation. It is the place of astral vision and psychic awareness.

4. Now, travel upon the path to the sphere of Tiphereth.

5. Tiphereth is the Kabbalistic world of balance and beauty. It has a golden hue and is synergistic with the Sun. This is the world of sacrificial gods and healing gods.

6. Now, visualize yourself as ascending even higher to the path that connects Tiphareth and Keter.

7. Keter is the world of unity. The Crown. The very top of the tree of life. All things of the universe is created here first in the world of spirit. It is here you may see the angelic hosts called *Chaioth ha Qadesh* (Holy Living Creatures).

8. Metatron may appear as an angelic being of flame and light. But, be open to him appearing as something else entirely.

9. Take a moment to speak with him. Ask him questions that you would like.

10. When you are finished go back down to Tiphereth then to Yesod, then back down to Malkuth.

11. Return to the physical plane and waking consciousness. Journal your experience.

Witchblood of The Fallen Angels

In some Traditional Witchcraft circles, it is believed that witches came from the union between The Grigori and the daughters of men. They became those of the "witchblood", a dark sangreal. When the children of the Watchers were born, their fathers taught them the magical mysteries of Heaven. They were taught the arts of astrology, herbology, magick, spells, root workings, signs and omens, and many other categories of witchcraft. The power of the angels was past through their blood and gave them many abilities. In Christian theology, if magick or the ability to grant miracles did not come from God or Jesus, then the only other explanation for magick would be the work of Satan or his demons.

When we look at the fallen Watchers and the Nephilim we may have the inclination to see them as demons. However, we would be making a mistake by seeing them in black and white. Yes, the Watchers were punished for their crimes against God, but they are not considered demons. They are more complicated than that. If we believe that the creator of all things, or the Judeo-Christian God, is omnipotent and infallible, then God does not make mistakes. I personally believe that he knew the Watchers would fall and lust after mortal women. He knew what that would mean. He wanted mortals to learn magick, just like he wanted Eve to eat of the Apple of Knowledge. It is unfortunate that even though he wanted this to be so, the Watchers had to still be punished. After all, even though God knew their nature, they still had to be punished otherwise all of creation may one day rise up against him. When we look at stories and mythologies we have to look at the bigger picture. Will the triumphs and failures bring change and spiritual evolution in the world? Or perhaps we truly are God's grand experiment. Perhaps God is the master scientist who puts the universe and its inhabitants in curious positions and circumstances simply just to see what would happen.

Witches of angelic blood, I find, are more inclined to work with astrology, the heavenly spheres, the stars, angels, and the powers of the gods. They are one with the heavens and have wondrous powers that can help mankind, if they so wish. No, I do not believe that all witches are from the fallen angels. Some witches get their powers from the gods, the land, elves, Fey, and/or the ancestors.

Journeying and Summoning Angels

One of the most profound experiences with Angelic Magick is to journey to meet the spirit in the astral and to conjure them in your ritual space. Before any spirit conjuration, it is wise to journey to their realm and meet them where they live. It is always more polite when someone comes to see you and gets to know you before they, out of the blue, ask you for a favor or advice. When you journey to meet the spirits, this will open a dialogue with them and they will be more apt to answer your call of summoning and will be more willing to help you. By journeying to them, you will also learn to tune in better to their energies. This will also help you when you summon them into your ritual space. It will also help you to make sure that the correct spirit has answered your call because you will be familiar with their energy signature. When summoning a spirit, it is more than just words that bring the spirit to you. You have to visualize the spirit, tune in to their energy signature, and ask them to come to you.

Upperworld conjurations such as with angel and planetary magick are different then lower spirit and demon summoning. Lower spirits and demons have chaotic energies and you have to control them through magical bindings and warning if they get out of hand. With spirits with a higher frequency, such as angels and planetary spirits, we are not forcing them to come into our space to help us with magick. We are asking them. By developing a relationship with a spirit they will want to help you. Remember, as well, that the spirit may want something in return for their aid in magick. They may want an offering of some kind or would like you to do a task for them. Never promise a spirit that you will do something and not do it. That being said, if a spirit asks you to do something unethical or illegal, it is better to decline. You can let the spirit know that you are unwilling to do their task and to ask them something else. I have found that planetary spirits and angels rarely ask for offerings, but when they do it is something you can easily do for them.

In order to evoke an angelic, planetary, or other Upperworld spirit to visible appearance you will need to do a few steps first. The first thing you will need to do is journey to the sephiroth where they dwell on the kabbalistic Tree of Life. Once we find them, we will want to ask the spirit if they are willing to work with us. If the answer is yes, then we can get to know them better in the astral plane. Once we do that, the next magical operation we should do is evoke them into a scrying device such as a crystal ball, scrying bowl, or magick mirror. The scrying tool is helpful aid when learning to see a spirit in the astral. After our clairvoyance abilities become strengthened we will not need the scrying device.

Evoking Angels into the Crystal Ball or Scrying Mirror

One way to work with the angelic beings is to evoke them into a crystal ball or other scrying device such as a crystal, obsidian mirror or sphere, magick mirror, or scrying bowl. My personal favorite is the crystal ball. I use one that is slightly smaller than my fist because it is easily moveable and inexpensive. You may use anything that works. The trick is that whatever scrying device you use needs to feel sacred, magical, and powerful. It is not about how expensive something is, but rather, how it puts your mind and spirit into a place of magick.

The items needed are: Crystal ball or scrying device, frankincense (or sage), a sensor, charcoal, a table or altar.

1. Place your crystal ball or other scrying device on an altar or table. An everyday coffee table works well.

2. Place yourself in a magical state of mind and a light trance.

3. Place the frankincense or sage in the sensor and light.

4. You may say the following words or come up with something on your own "Great Archangel (name of archangel). We ask that you appear within the crystal sphere (or other scrying device) and grant us with your presence and wisdom."

5. Scry into the device and wait to see the archangel. You may only see a faint image or fog. This is ok. Use your intuition and intuit if the archangel has appeared. In time, with practice, the angel will appear more clearly.

6. Spend some time speaking with the archangel and asking questions. It may help to use a voice recorder to record the messages.

7. Thank the archangel and bid farewell.

Melek Taus

Melek Taus is the Peacock Angel of the Yezidi people. The Yezidi are originally from the area of Iran, Iraq, and Syria, however now they can be found all over Europe and in the United States. The beliefs of the Yezidi was originally an oral tradition but they did have two important books. One book is named *Mishefa Resh* which translates to *The Black Book* and the other is called *Kiteb-i Cilwe* which means *The Book of Revelation*. These books are believed to have been written between the 12th and 14th Centuries CE. It seems that these holy books are a later

addition to the religious tradition and not many of the Yezidi have a copies.

Yezidi is thought to translate to "The People of the Angel", but no one actually knows. They believe themselves to be the oldest religion of the Middle East and it was not until they were persecuted and killed by Muslims and Christians that they became small in numbers. They worship a Peacock Angel named Melek Taus, or some of the Yezidi people called him, Tawasi Melek. In their cosmology, God created a white pearl that was to be the seed of all creation. He then created seven angels to take the pearl seed and create the heavens and the earth; Tawasi Melek was the most powerful and skillful of the seven angels and became their leader. When God created man, Tawasi Melek refused to bow down before him because he only loved God and could not bow down to anyone other than God himself. Because of Tawasi Melek's great love for God, God made him the leader of the seven angels. The Yezidi pray and honor Tawasi Melek as the leader of the angels and the avatar of God, much like how Christians honor Jesus.

One of the main reasons that the Yezidi people are persecuted by Muslims and Christians is because the angel that they pray to has similar attributes to their Satan. According to the Yezidi, Tawasi Melek is sometimes referred to as Azazel. In Muslim belief, Azazel is the adversary of God himself, the great angel who we call Satan. Birul Acikyildiz, in her book *The Yezidis: The History of a Community, Culture, and Religion* says, "According to Muslim tradition, it was the peacock that helped Satan to enter Paradise and seduce Adam and Eve into eating the forbidden fruit. Therefore, the peacock is identified with Satan."

To the Yezidi people, the peacock is a symbol of beauty, magick, and the divine. They see Tawasi Melek as the great redeemer of humanity and the divine because he himself had to be redeemed. In some Yezidi myths, Tawasi Melek was banished from heaven and condemned to walk the earth alone. He was heart broken to be away from his beloved God so he cried for 7,000 years. Through this act, he was redeemed by God and allowed back in heaven.

Some of the Yezidi believe that the fall and redemption of Tawasi Melek was planned and ordained by God himself. If we take the idea that God is the Grand Master Designer of the Universe and he knows all things past, present, and future and nothing happens without his consent, then it was his plan to have Tawasi Melek fall from grace for 7,000 years. In this thought, God wanted man to spiritually evolve and this could only happen if there was adversary in the world. In other words, the expulsion from Paradise had to happen so that humans could have the freedom of Will. If they stayed in Paradise then the human race would only be a sort of pet to god and never a creation in his own image; the master of his/her destiny and creator of their own Divine Will on earth.

Lucifer

Lucifer means "The Bright One" or the "Bringer of the dawn". He received this title because he is considered the most beautiful and powerful of all the angels. No other angel was ranked above him and he sat beside the throne of God. In Christian myth, Lucifer, like Tawasi Melek, refused to bow down before man and started a war in heaven against God. Because of his betrayal, he and his followers were banished from heaven. There are many similarities to the myth of Tawasi Melek and Lucifer. It is believed that Christianity borrowed the Yezidi myth and made it their own. Again, in some Christian, as well as gnostic thought, God needed someone to challenge humans so that they would have free will and the opportunity to become more spiritually evolved. God chose Lucifer to be the scapegoat and the challenger of man.

In some spiritual philosophies, Lucifer is the dark hero who teaches humans how to become their own spiritual saviors and question divine authority. In the myth of Lilith and Adam from Jewish texts, it was Lilith who gave women the free will not to be subdued by man. Also the serpent, who is thought to be the disguise of Lucifer, convinced Eve to go against god and eat the forbidden fruit. Because of this, Eve was the one who gave all humans after her free will and the ability to make choices of their own. When we look at these myths through a spiritual lense we see that Lucifer is a sort of champion of the human race. Yes, it is taught in Judeo-Christianity that Lucifer's motives were to get revenge on god, but through doing so, humans now have the ability to think and question things for themselves. This means question authority.

Question traditional norms; especially if they have become stagnant and have outlived their usefulness. In this regard, Lucifer takes on similar characteristics as the Greco-Roman Prometheus, the Titan who gave fire (technology) to man. He literally gave the fires of heaven to the people of earth so they could be on a more equal footing to the gods. This is what Lucifer as done; he gives men and women the "light" so that they make informed decisions for themselves.

In gnostic spirituality, "light from heaven" means the illumination of that which was once hidden. The ability to see spirituality in all its forms and not become strapped down to old traditions and dogma. If we look at patriarchal religions, some of the old dogma says it is ok to own slaves and women are not equal to men. This thinking subjugates others and only serves men who do not wish to share authority and power. Entities such as Lucifer and Tawasi Melek teach to challenge these ideas and that power does not belong to just a few. The Creator of the Universe never intended for humans or any other species in the Universe not to question and seek to understand the world around us. The Creator, or God, created life so that they could have a deeper understanding of experience in many different forms. If we return to the belief that God wanted Lucifer to be the scapegoat, then questioning religious authority is not evil, it is divine.

In some Traditional Witchcraft circles, Lucifer in honored as a great spirit of light and enlightenment. He is not associated with the Christian Devil or Satan. He is an angelic being who, through his illumination, shows us what is hidden in the darkness. His light shines through our soul and our being to bring into light our darkest fears so that we may face them. As the saying goes, "where there is fear, there is great power." He also shows us the world how it truly is. Sometimes we romanticize our lives and the world around us. Lucifer shows us our strengths, as well as our weaknesses. This helps us to see the reality of our lives, not how we wish it could be. Lucifer also is the bridge between the celestial angelic realm and the physical plane. He was once stood next to the throne of God, but now rules earth instead. He retains his angelic powers, but they are transmitted to the powers over the physical world. He can be seen as a link between humans and angels. Perhaps that is why he is so feared by the patriarchy. In Judeo-Christian belief, to be human is to be flawed , but to be angelic is to be perfect. They see Lucifer as the flawed angel who was banished to earth. They forget how he is the one who gave us wisdom and free will.

The powers of Lucifer can teach us how to gain wisdom and free will. He can teach us how to challenge authority that is repressing the people. He can show us how to look deep into our hearts and minds and see the darkness within, so that we may see what lies beneath the glamour we have built for ourselves. When we do this, we can make changes in our lives so that we may go forward on our spiritual path. He can also teach us angelic magick that is practical for the physical plane. He can also give us the gift of inspiration so that we may continue to walk our path even through times of darkness.

Journey To Meet Lucifer/ Tawasi Melek

1. Chose a time when the morning or evening star (Venus) is visible in the sky. This will be at either dawn or dusk.

2. Light incense that will tune your senses to the Light bringer. You may use Sage, Frankincense, Dragon's Blood, Rosemary, Coriander, or any scent that reminds you of illumination and light.

3. State your intention to meet Lucifer or Tawasi Melek. Journey to the morning or evening Star.

4. Lucifer or Tawasi Malek may appear as an angel of light, a peacock, a being of fire, or something completely different. Do not judge your experience.

5. Spend some time getting to know him and ask him questions. This is a good being to ask about your own spirituality or how you can change things in your life that has become "old and dogmatic". You may ask him about the challenges in your life and how to overcome them.

6. When you are ready, return to your body.

7. If you feel called to do so, leave offerings for Lucifer or Tawasi Melek.

Luciferian Ritual of Awakening

This ritual calls upon Lucifer to awaken your spirit and psychic abilities. It is not a invocation, but an empowering from the angelic being. Items needed: small cauldron or fireproof dish, isopropyl alcohol, or a liquor that is suitable for burning. Matches. An offering to Lucifer

Ritual:

1. In a darkened room, place ritual items before you. Give your offering to Lucifer, saying, "*Lucifer, bright shining one. Please accept this offering. May you grant me your powers this night.*"

2. Meditate on Lucifer. See him in your mind. See the Angel of light that you saw upon your journey with him. What did you learn about him when you journeyed to him? Remember the insights and magick that he taught you.

3. Pore a small amount of isopropyl alcohol or liquor in your cauldron or fire proof vessel. Light it and gaze into the flame saying,

"I summon Lucifer, the angel of light. You who fills me with inspiration. Redeemer of man. You who lights the way upon my spiritual path. I summon you, lucifer into this flame. As this flame fills the room with brightness, so, too, does your power fill my spirit."

4. Visualize Lucifer in his glory in the flame.

5. In your heart, have a great longing to merge with the powers of Lucifer.

6. Breathe in Lucifer into your Root Chakra, *"May Lucifer light the path I tread on the earthly plain."*

7. Breathe in Lucifer into your Navel Chakra, *"May Lucifer inspire me to create my own destiny upon my path."*

8. Breathe in Lucifer into your Solar Plexus Chakra, *"May Lucifer help me discover my Divine Will."*

9. Breathe in Lucifer into your Heart Chakra, *"May Lucifer fill my heart with compassion for those who travel the path along side of me."*

10. Breathe in Lucifer into your Throat Chakra, *"May Lucifer show me how to speak my truth and see through the illusions of society."*

11. Breathe in Lucifer into your Brow Chakra, *"May Lucifer bring me visions of the celestial realms."*

12. Breath in Lucifer into your Crown Chakra, *"May Lucifer open my spirit so that I may find enlightenment."*

13. Feel the angelic powers of Lucifer coursing through your energy bodies. Allow the flames to dissipate. Say your thanks to Lucifer and journal your experience.

14. Pay attention to any dreams, omens, or signs you may have the next few days.

Evocation of the Angels

Angels have been summoned for magick, wisdom, and gnosis for thousands of years. They are known as luminaries, devas, higher spirits, and messengers of god. We know that each angel has an energy or phenomenon that they control or govern. Summoning the angels is one of the most powerful techniques in magick. There are many books on Solomon's magick and Enochian magick that give you specific formulas to call down and even force an angel to appear before you in your magical temple. These specific texts are a part of medieval and Renaissance magick. Let us take a moment to understand this type of magick and how it works and even how it does not work.

In Medieval times, the Christian Church prevailed with its tortures and constant threat of death to witches and heretics. Anyone caught performing magick that was not a "miracle" of Jesus was sentenced to death. Magicians, at that time, bought into the rhetoric that anything that was not "of God" was evil at worst, chaotic at best, and could be controlled by the words of God. However, the evocation of angels was not seen as heretical in the eyes of Medieval and Renaissance magicians. They believed the wisdom and magick of the angels to be God's gift to mankind. After all, in some Judeo-Christian myths, God commanded the angels to bow down before man. The knowledge and power of angels was thought to improve the spiritual advancement of the human race. Some magicians felt that the angels "owed" their knowledge to them.

The path of the shaman, healer, mystic, and witch do not share the same view as the magicians of the past. Angelic evocation is a practice that is considered sacred and should be treated as a gift from the angels. As I am constantly saying, the spirits do not owe us anything. We do not disrespect spirits and we do not command them. What we do, instead, is come into a partnership with them. Unlike other spirits, angels do not ask for gifts or offerings for their services. The only thing they may ask of you is to use their power wisely and for the advancement of yourself and your community. Yes, you can ask the angels to help you obtain personal desires, but most of the angels are concerned with the greater good of the Universe. Again, It is always better to come into a partnership with a spirit. This way, they are acting in accord to their will and will not try to get out of the contract or binding nor will they give you what you want in the least desirable way. Think getting money from someone who just died.

Evoking Angels for magick is very similar to evoking planetary spirits. The formula is pretty much the same. When you contact the angels, remember that they will be true to their nature. For example, if you evoke the archangel Raphael, he is better suited for things that are related to healing, communication, magick, and the element of air. He can do much more than this but these are the basics. When you evoke the angel to your temple space, you will want to evoke using the angelic sigil. This acts as a signature or a magical key that will help your consciousness tune into the energies of that angel. If you do not know the angelic sigil you can ask the angel in question to show you a symbol or sigil that is best to call them with. When you have the angel's sigil or symbol you can astrally draw it over your scrying device. You can also take something erasable, such as an eyeliner pencil and physically draw the sigil on your magick mirror or scrying device. Once you have evoked the angel into your temple space you can ask him questions about his abilities and wisdom. When you become proficient at evoking the angel into your device, you may can evoke the angel into your temple space without the aide of a scrying device. Use the Kabbalistic correspondence on page 188 The Planets Chapter for days of the week. The day of the week should correspond with the correct sephiroth. For Lucifer/ Melek

Taus use either Sunday, Tuesday, or Saturday

Evocation of Angels To Visible Appearance

You can use the evocation below to summon archangels, angels, Watchers, Nephilim, Lucifer, or Melek Taus.

1. Decide on the angel you would like to conjure/summon

2. On the correct planetary day of the week, prepare your ritual space. If you need the Triangle and skyring tool (mirror, bowl, crystal ball) set up these tools now. If you are using a magick mirror, draw the spirit's sigil on the mirror using a black eyeliner pencil.

3. Light the colored candle that corresponds with the appropriate sephiroth of the angel. You may use one or two candles and place them near the triangle of art. Light incense that corresponds with the angel's sephiroth. If you are unsure simply use frankincense.

4. Aspect your god or goddess. Allow yourself to feel the power of your god in your body but make sure you are mostly in control so that you may do the conjuration.

5. If you are using a scrying bowl or crystal ball, astrally trace the angel's sigil over the ball or bowl.

6. Summon the angel with these words, or you may come up with words of your own. *"I summon (name of angel) in the name of (god you invoked and any powers of wondrous deeds they have done). (Angel name), come and appear before me and speak to me in a clear and tangible voice. I ask that you show yourself to me visibly (In this scrying tool if using) ."*

7. Allow the angel a moment to manifest. You can aid this by connecting to the energies of the sephiroth where the angel lives and

visualizing its appearance before you. The spirit can use the visualization as a tool to manifest. If the spirit has not manifested, place more incense on the burner and repeat the summoning.

8. When the spirit has manifested say, *"(Name of Angel), I welcome you into my ritual space and thank you for coming. I would like to (state your intention)"*

9. You may now ask the spirit questions, ask for help with magick, or ask them to help you perform a task.

10. When you are finished with the summoning say, *"(Angel Name), thank you for helping me with (intention/ magick/ etc). I hope you will come again and work with me in the art of magick. Thank you. Farewell."*

11. See the spirit fading away. Extinguish the candles and incense.

12. Cleanse or banish your working space.

6
Higher Beings

Quetzalcoatl (Aztec)

Quetzalcoatl was a priest-King of the Toltec people. He was a wise ruler who provided his people with many things. He taught them how to plant crops and he was a master craftsman. He took sanctuary in his temple and would not go out very often to see his people. In his temple he would often do penance to the gods. For the good of the people, it was customary to perform human sacrifice, but he would not do so. He would only sacrifice birds, snakes, and butterflies.

The priests of the kingdom grew tired of Quetzalcoatl not performing the obligatory human sacrifices so they decided to banish him from the land. They would trick him into doing it himself. The priests came to Quetzalcoatl's temple with a mirror and showed him how he really looked. He looked monstrous!

"I cannot go outside!" Said Quetzalcoatl.

"We will help you!" Said the priests. "We will make you a grand mask and costume." The priests made him a turquoise and feather mask and costume for him to wear. Quetzalcoatl was pleased and went walking among the people.

While he was out, the priests created a potion that would make Quetzalcoatl quite drunk. When he returned they gave him this potion. They gave him four drinks and one more. Poor Quetzalcoatl was so drunk he forgot to do penance and sacrifices to the gods. He remained drunk the entire night. When the sun rose in the morning, Quetzalcoatl was quite ashamed of his behavior. Very unfitting for a priest-King. In his humiliation, he banished himself from the kingdom. He had great sorrow for his embarrassment. In disparity, he set himself a flame and cremated himself. Instead of smoke and ashes, birds flew up to the heavens. The priest saw his heart rise from the ground and rise up to the heavens to become the Morning Star. From then forth, Quetzalcoatl was known as the Lord of the Dawn.

Ascended Masters

The Ascended Masters are human spirits that have spiritually evolved to the point that they are no longer bound by reincarnation and the wheel of life, death, and rebirth. As we have talked about before, the Universe wants us to spiritually evolve. In Kabbalistic cosmology, the source of all things, that which we call God, wanted to become more than it was and wanted to have experiences rather than simply be the One Omnipotent deity. It wanted to know itself. One cannot know oneself without the reflection of others and having experiences. With this, all creatures must evolve as well. Life on earth has taken millions of years to evolve to where we are now and we have many more years to go. There are those who have evolved spiritually to such a place that they no longer need to be reborn on earth to continue their lessons. Perhaps they are a very ancient soul that has been on earth for many many lifetimes. Perhaps they simply made the choice to evolve faster than others. Only they can say.

Let's talk a moment about the Buddhist concept of *Liberation*. This means that the spirit of a person has learned all of their earthly lessons and has no more karma attached to their spirit. According to Buddhist cosmology, when we have karma attached to us it acts as an energetic anchor that pulls us back to the earthly plane so that we may resolve that karma. This is not a punishment, but rather an opportunity to evolve into higher spiritual beings. Once we have evolved to a higher spiritual state, we are no longer bound to return to physical form to be reborn. This is not an easy task and there are sacrifices and hard choices to be made. Once a person has become liberated they may choose how to spend eternity. Even in spiritual evolution there are choices to be made. You may join with the godhead, or Brahma, and merge your being with that of the creator of all things. The other choice is to remain close to the godhead but continue on in full awareness of your individuality in a state of bliss, or Nirvana. Another choice is to become an Ascended Master or a Spiritual Teacher for humanity.

There are many Ascended Masters that have been channeled by psychics, prayed to for healing, and meditated upon for enlightenment. Some of the more famous ones are The Buddha, St. Germain, and Saints. I have also seen where some people refer to pagan gods and goddesses as, not deities, but Ascended Masters who took the form of gods in order to better teach humanity. As a pagan, healer, and teacher, I can say wholeheartedly that the gods are deities in their own right and are not Ascended Masters in disguise. They feel and communicate differently and have different powers. It is said that Ascended Masters were very powerful and knowledgeable in life. They may have been shamans, spiritual teachers, magicians, monks, are some other magical person. Some of the characteristics they have in common are never aging, magick, great selflessness, knowledge in science and spirituality, alchemy, divination, and healing abilities.

There are other Ascended Masters that may or not be so famous. I personally am working with Reiki Masters, in spirit, who I would consider Ascended Masters. I call them Ascended Reiki Masters. These are Reiki Masters who used the healing powers of Reiki and continue to use their healing abilities after death in the astral or spirit world. When someone is attuned to Reiki there energies, chakras, and meridians are "programmed" to channel the Reiki healing energies in a direct way. Before any healing, we say a prayer to Grand Master Dr. Usui, Grand

Master Takata, and other deceased Reiki Masters to help channel, direct, and aid in our client's healing experience.

When I first was attuned to Reiki back in 2006 I was doing a reiki healing for a client. Anyone who knows me knows that when it comes to magick, healing, or anything shamanistic I easily trance out. All of a sudden I was aware of a spiritual presence in the room with me. I opened my eyes to see a short Asian man dressed in a ruby red silk robe with gold embroidery. He was silent. I asked him his name and he simply replied, "I am a Reiki Master in spirit who will help you on your path of Reiki." Every time I perform a reiki healing, or anytime I do any healing really, I call to Reiki Master to help me with healing my client.

When we work with Ascended Masters they do not have to be saints, reiki masters, or Buddhas. They can simply be those ascended spirits who wish to help and heal humanity. I feel it is better to have a personal relationship with such spiritual beings. Perhaps they will help you heal yourself or someone else. Perhaps they will guide you upon your spiritual path. It is better not to have too many expectations and limit the wondrous possibilities that the Ascended Masters can give to you.

Secret Chiefs and Hidden Masters

There is a belief in some spiritualist and ceremonial groups of cosmic adepts and rulers of the Universe. These are beings that help certain special magical humans in revealing the secrets of the Universe to a select few. From my research, it seems that the first mention of these enlightened beings were mentioned in Karl Von Eckartshausen in his book *The Cloud Upon the Sanctuary,* he says "...the society of the Elect, which had continued from the first day of creation to the present time; its members, it is true, are scattered all over the world, but they have always been united in the spirit and in one truth...This community of light has been called from all time the invisible celestial Church, or the most ancient of all communities…"

S.L. MacGregor Mathers believed that he was in communication with cosmic beings that he called "The Secret Chiefs". He believed, that because he was the founder and leader of the Hermetic Order of the Golden Dawn, they were transmitting to him magical secrets that would unlock great power for the Golden Dawn to use in their Second Order.

H.P. Blavatsky (1831-1891) was co-founder of the Theosophical Society and author of the books *Isis Unveiled* and *The Secret Doctrine*. She believed that she was in contact with "The Masters". These were spiritually evolved beings who lived all over the world who would communicate with her telepathically. Unlike most of the ascended masters, The Masters were not spirits, but actual human beings. The Masters gave her instructions throughout her life. She obeyed their direction when they ordered her to move to America, Tibet, India and many other places. When she journeyed to Tibet, it was documented that Blavatsky spent time in the physical company of The Masters. Other people had witnessed The Masters as well. They were said to appear and disappear in the blink of an eye and they could materialize hand written letters with their instructions written on them. The Masters were the most important thing in Blavatsky's life. They instructed her spiritual dedication, education, and helped her author her books. She looked to them for guidance her entire life. It was only *she* who had direct link to them in the Theosophical Society. Upon her death, her successors believed that they had obtained a direct link to them as well. But instead of describing them as living humans, they were later described as spiritual beings of light.

Aleister Crowley said that he was in contact with the being named *Aiwass*. When Crowley and his wife visited Cairo, this spirit dictated him the infamous, *The Book of the Law,* which was the inspiration for him to begin his Ordo Templi Orientis, in which is practiced the religious philosophy of Thelema. Thelema's main axiom is, "Do what thou Wilt shall be the whole of the Law. Love is the Law. Love under Will." In this spiritual practice, it is believed that every person on earth has a divine spiritual will and purpose on earth. Once you discover your cosmic Will, you will live a life of magick, meaning, and spiritual purpose.

Ascended Ancestors

The Ascended Ancestors are similar the Ascended Masters but instead of wanting to heal the universe and guide humanity to spiritual evolution, the primary goal of the Ascended Ancestors is to guide their bloodline on their spiritual path. The Ascended Ancestors are our ancestors who have lived life after life growing and evolving to a state of a higher spiritual elevation. When someone dies and goes to the Underworld, they go to a place of healing and rejuvenation. This is a place where they can be reunited with their deceased family and loved ones, and find much healing.

From a shamanic point of view, the dead do not go to heaven or the Upperworld. When they die, and their spirit leaves the physical body, they go down to the roots of the great tree of life to The Realm of the Dead. This is not a place of hell, but a wondrous place in the Otherworld where the dead can find happiness and peace. The Realm of the Dead is a beautiful place in the Underworld where there is much joy. Some say it is a mirror image of the physical world and there is not much difference in the buildings and landscapes of where you lived on the physical plane. Others say that it is a place in the energy world that is shaped by the collective thoughts of the ancestors. In my journeys to the Realm of the Dead, I have found both of these things to be true.

When our beloved dead are in the Underworld, they have the opportunity to heal and review their lives with the aid of other ancestors and healing helpers that help them upon their path. When the time is right, the ancestors may choose to reincarnate upon the physical plane. They will do this life after life until they reach a certain point in their evolution that they may stay in the Underworld as an ancestral teacher and guide or they may ascend to the Upperworld to become an ascended ancestor. I have heard this term as a Divine Ancestor. What this means is that the ancestors has spiritually evolved to a point where they are similar to gods. They have a divine duty to aid their bloodline as well as help in the evolution of the Universe.

I find that it is very beneficial to work with your Ascended Ancestor. He or she can guide you very quickly upon your path and give you wonderful wisdom and insights. I love working with my ancestors, but when you are working with the dead they have the same hopes, fears, desires, and prejudices as they did in life. They are a very powerful ally but they are also imperfect and fallible, just as any of us can be. The Ascended Ancestors have moved beyond those things. They are no longer interested in the things they were in life, but because they once were alive, they understand that we, their descendants, are imperfect and make mistakes. They have an emotional-spiritual investment in us that the Ascended Masters may or may not have. To me, the difference between the Ascended Masters and the Ascended Ancestors are that the Masters are our teachers where the Ancestors are our family.

Thunder Beings

Thunder Beings are Native American entities that live in the sky above the earth. They mostly manifest during thunder and lightning storms but they can manifest at any time during any type of weather. They have great healing powers and are often called upon during healing ceremonies. They appear to be very bright like lightning. Native American shamans often ask for a Thunder Being to live in their drum for the purpose of healing. In Native belief, one never forces a spirit into a magical object. As magical people, Native Americans live in harmony with all spirits and one spirit or life form in not more sacred than another. Everyone has a sacred part in the Universe; however, we may ask a spirit to help us for healing. There is the belief that if a being no longer chooses to live in the drum for any reason, it will leave in a thunderous boom ripping the drum.

The best time to connect with the Thunder Beings is, of course, during a lightning storm. This is not the only time you can work with these beings. You work with them during any type of weather day or night. To visit them, astral project out of your body and ask your totem to take you to the land of the Thunder Beings in the clouds.

Exercise: Meeting The Ascended Master, Divine Ancestors, and Thunder Beings

1. Astral project yourself, to the World Tree.

2. Ask your totem to accompany you.

3. Ask your totem to take you to an Ascended Master, Ascended Ancestor or one of the Thunder Beings.

4. Follow your totem up the tree branches to your destination.

5. Be open to what the landscape looks like. This is the home of the

Higher Being you are looking for.

6. Introduce yourself to the Higher Being and ask them if they are willing to help you upon your path.

7. Return the way you came and journal your experiences.

Interview With Billie Topa Tate

The Native American community works with celestial and Upperworld spirits. These higher beings are called to be present in healing ceremonies for the betterment and healing for all. Billie Topa Tate is my Native American and Reiki Teacher whom I admire and respect a great deal. Below, is an interview I had with her in the Spring of 2017.

Chris Allaun: Billie, can you tell us a little bit about yourself and where you learned about your Native tradition and about the spirits?

Billie Topa Tate: My name is Billie Topa Tate. I'm Mescalero Apache and a (spiritual) teacher. When I was about 11 years old, my mother, Momma Little Wolf, decided to have me go outside of the tribe for energy training. And so before that time it was predominantly Native American training, education, and ceremony. Our particular platform is our oral tradition. There is really very few things written down and that's why we take time to share that with our families; our stories, our ceremonies, and also our deeper connections to our teachers in spirit and all the wonderful beings who assist us in good and loving ways. We are guided by their wonderful energies. I have been doing this for a long long time. I have my practice here in Evanston, Illinois, and I have opened a center called MSI Wellness Center. We have been doing this for 19 years on a formal platform outside of the tribe. Before that time, working for the first holistic and integrative wellness center in the state of Illinois with Dr. Edelberg and a lot of other wonderful doctors. It was really wonderful to be able to share this information with people outside of the tribe.

The training starting officially before I was 11 years old and my wonderful teachers were first my mother and father who I regarded as very gentle giants. I would watch them and observe how they would interact with the environment. We would be walking home in the desert from a long day of harvesting and making connections with the environment. When the sun was setting, my father and mother would put everything down and do what is called A Sunset Ceremony. The first part which is a Sunrise Ceremony which is very similar where we start our day by having gratitude, then by activating our consciousness to our great purpose and also that we are very happy to be walking this earth and happy to connect with all the sentient beings here. Sunrise and sunset were done everyday and I observed how they would wonderfully connect with all of those energies. As I progressed my mother and father really taught me a lot about using natural things which we call *indigenous wellness* to maintain the integrity of our good health; physically, emotionally, mentally, and spiritually, and at all other levels. My mother was a wonderful healer and my father was a wonderful healer. I remember one day, my father was getting ready to go out and harvest just a little bit of cactus and things of that nature, which is very medicinal. Someone came with a very sick child that was in our small community. What he did is he placed his hands together and really went inward and I saw his energy field become very bright and I saw all of these wonderful energies around him like these spheres of light and also divine helpers. Then he started to sweep the energy field of this child with this hands just about five inches above the child's body and just started gently sweeping the energy field because she was very fidgety, she was very tired, she wasn't feeling good because she had a little bit of a fever. As he started sweeping the energy field she became more calm and then started to fall asleep. Without even touching the child he started to project this beautiful white light into her energy field and balanced all the chakras. Doing so really helped her to facilitate wellness. I saw all the divine helpers assist this process by sending the energy through him. Then he was completed and he went into a state of gratitude and then he gave the child back to her father. I was sitting there in total amazement. This was the time for me, at that very young age, to have that pivotal time when I said I want to do that. I want to understand who these beautiful beings are and I want to understand the energy that he generated by doing this. He didn't make a big deal out of it. He finished with it then he went on to go harvest cactus. It was just a very matter of fact thing. I thought, this is amazing! I want very much to do this. Of course, the father was very filled with gratitude when he saw his child, not just peaceful, but in a state of balance, which you can see in the energy field that was around the child. It was very fascinating.

Even before I was 11 years old I was receiving training just by observing them and asking questions about what transpired. Even the herbs that they used are still standing the test of time. I use them all the time with my practice and myself because they will always do what they do. They are very good against sickness and viruses. I learned a lot about those things also. I moved into another traditional platform of dream time work, understanding the life journey of a person, identifying points of origin, limitations that people might have. These are they things you may learn as you progress because with Native American medicine families, which is what I was born into, what we do is we astrologically have a deep understanding of when a child comes into this world what they're supposed to be doing. The first female born is given to the service work and also to develop the skills to have psychic energies and also to understand how the universal principles work. There are all of these things you start to receive from the time of birth. It's a wonderful experience.

So as I progressed and started learning from other Native American teachers it was time for me to move outside of the arena of the native ceremonies and my mother told me that it would be a good idea to learn from the Tibetans. What I found when I did that is that we have very similar understandings about how the universe works and also with the Creator has given us. As Native people we use the drumming ceremonies because their sound actually allows for a bridge of energy to occur from the physical aspect to all the levels of energy so that's why drumming is very important, and sound, we use vocables when we do drumming and the Tibetans would use mantras and different kinds of sounds like the horn and bells, we do a little bit of that also. I found that to be a very similar quality. The principles of the Tibetans are very similar in our philosophies and our ceremonies, which is very interesting. As time went on I learned a lot of different things in perspective to their work as well because they do have the Chinese herbs and the Tibetan herbs that they would use as well. Having said that I have been trained since the time of birth to really work on my purpose, which is to be a spiritual teacher. To be a Native American mentor for our people and also for people outside of the tribe as well.

CA: Who are the Holy Medicine People and how do we work and connect with them in a simplified way?

BTT: The Holy Medicine People were the original medicine people who are in the energy world and they launched a platform with the Creator that had a commitment that they would help and assist in service work despite the persecutions of the people. According to the stories , they were talking with the creator and that time, entirely possible to talk with the Creator and also the divine helpers that are there. We had an understanding that people who were less aware would have qualities that were aggressive, violent, or opinionated, and things of that nature. It was our goal to be of service to provide medicine. Medicine would be to interact with all people, to provide what we could for their survival, for their enlightenment. That was their commitment. In the energy world the Holy Medicine People hold space for our ceremonies. For example, when we do the medicine wheel ceremony, on the four directions we have these beautiful medicine helpers to hold the space for the four directions and that's why we have these songs to activate the four directions, to activate the medicine of the four directions, and also to activate the opportunity to connect with these wonderful Holy Medicine People that are in the energy world and, of course, any of the other Medicine Elders that transition to the other side; when they "pass away". They are brought into the roles and responsibilities to hold the spaces in the energy world for healing medicine to occur. Also for guidance and mentorship to the elders that are here and all the other people who would like very much to participate in the mentorship which means being of service on the planet and enlightening and awakening ourselves on the earth to be of service to others. Being of service means to provoke a level of awareness, to interact and intervene to provoke healing. That particular platform of the Holy Medicine People is always being repopulated or populated even more by the elders that transcend and go into the other side. When they go on the other side their physical bodies are gone but the essence of who they are and their consciousness and the energy that they carry is still present and will always be there. Our goal is to be able to be in our spirit enough to receive their energy and their guidance as much as possible.

To connect with the Holy Medicine People, one of the things I recommend is to be in that place of spirit, and that means meditation. Meditation is a very important tool because it allows us to be guided by higher thought and also to get connected to a higher quality of thinking and also a higher quality of our presence. That all gets launched by having a quiet moment. Meditation for an hour or half an hour is going to help us to really get connected to our guides, our divine helpers, our higher self, and to be able to ask questions and to be able to wall with them. It doesn't get any better than that. We also need to come back into this world and implement some of those things for ourselves and others. When we meditate we are going into a place where we are getting connected to a higher aspect of our thinking. When we become one with all things in that meditation platform our vibration gets to the point we can hear them (the Holy Medicine People) that much more. I feel, for most people, they will connect with them through a knowing first; a thought, which is easy to do in the consciousness, so having a sacred intention is going to be very important before we go into meditation.

The first thing we want to do is set an intention. In order to create a sacred intention we must have a little bit of quiet time. Morning is always best for me because I like to get up at 4:30 in the morning and meditate. My guides, my higher self, and my virtuous teachers in spirit know that they can speak to me very clearly at 4:30 in the morning but then throughout the day also. When I'm sitting in meditation I am wanting to go within my heart. The heart chakra is in this world and also in the other world. The world of healing, the world of enlightenment, the world of miracles. This comes from being in the center of the heart chakra. So when we go inward to create a sacred intention, we are going to go into our heart with our consciousness and be in the center of that place with a request or a question or some aspect of enlightenment we are looking for, or quality we are looking for. We are going to express that by asking for our higher self and our wonderful teachers in spirit and our Holy Medicine People to be present and also to facilitate and answer to a question that we may have and then we will begin by saying, "By the power of our good merits." Then we go inward and we ask for our Holy Medicine People to be present, to assist us in a resolution or insight. Then we present our request. When we present our request we end it with a gratitude statement because it adjust our energy field to receive it. Then we go into sacred breath. This is a calming breath and a breath that we can connect to everything in a good way. Then we go into that quiet place. You can stay in the quiet place as long you like; I recommend 20 minutes. Then express gratitude.

CA: Who are the Angels that we work with for healing?

BTT: In the Native Tradition we have a word that represents angels, "luminaries". Enlightened beings. There are different levels of them. Just like if you would look at a good successful business. There are different kinds of roles and responsibilities and qualities. Different tasks that the Universe would need. The highest order is the archangels. They have been around since the beginning of the creation of our Universe. They know the science of it and have been given gifts to help to coordinate other things in this world. Archangel Michael's name means "He who is like God." Michael helped the Creator create the universe. He knows the floor plan, so to speak, of the universe that the Creator made. Archangel Raphael, his name means "He who is like God's medicine". That is why Raphael is called upon by doctors and healing people. This is because he represents medicine that God gives. Archangel Uriel holds the beginning of the gate, or bridge, from the form and the formless. They are pretty powerful beings. They have a quality about them that is incredibly blissful. But as a human being when you encounter even an essence of that energy, you know that the energy is extremely powerful. They are in beautiful columns of light. They exist everywhere, but they have a particular place that they go to assess what is needed to be done. It is the place of light. This place of light is filled with different vibrations and different shades of light and colors of light. And all of the light is used by them to utilize in their work. There are different levels of angels; healing angels, angels that help transition, angels that help with people after transition, angels that walk the earth to secure the vitality of the sunrise and sunset occur, earth angels, sun angels, then there are the building elements that people see often. These are sometimes seen in photographs as little white orbs. They are called the "lapikas". The lapikas are small little angels that work to develop something. It could be a plant or the birth of a child. We see them a lot in nature and in our ceremonies.

CA: If we want to connect with the angels or if we, ourselves, needs some healing, How can we best call upon them?

BTT: There is a story that the Creator gave us the gift of consciousness. That consciousness is connected to your focus. If your focus is here then your consciousness is here, but you can use your consciousness to go anywhere. You can go to Mars, you can go to the Hall of Wisdom. When you are asleep your consciousness goes to different places. The story goes that the Creator gave us this gift of consciousness and the purpose of this gift was, one of the reasons, was to access the other worlds. We can access the worlds of angels or we can access the world of Reiki or we can access the world of healing , the world of wisdom, but we can also access the world of limitations and judgement.

Through our intention we can channel a connection through our express desire to one of the worlds. My teacher used to say, "Suker unto them and they Suker unto you." What that means is that when we acknowledge them and we ask for their help and we thank them for their help and we encourage them more to be in our life. We are establishing a relationship. Any relationship that's healthy and good is vitalized on a daily basis.

One way to work with the angels is to go to your heart center and say, "By the power of my good merits, I invoke for my virtuous higher self, all the wonderful beings who assist me in good and loving ways." Then you can list out the archangels and your personal angels to be present and to assist you to answer a question and provide healing qualities to you. And you always want to say, "physically, emotionally, mentally, spiritually and at all other levels". Because if you don't say that then you might only receive it on a spiritual realm. It is important to give the angels permission to intervene at those levels and provide healing at those levels or give you insight at those levels. Then you state what it is you are asking for or state what it is that you need. The final thing is to express gratitude. You always express gratitude. When you are finished just have a quiet moment on focusing on the breath and then let go. You are also going to ask for your angels, your personal angels or the archangels to provide you with some healing energies during sleep time.

CA: How do the Native American people view the stars?

BTT: Everything is symbolic because the Creator as given us the understanding of what's called universal symbols. The Universe speaks in symbols. It's the first language of the universe and the only language of the Universe. We understand that the Creator talks to us through symbolic representation of things. For example, when there is a very light rain we know that the universe is telling us that this is a blessing rain. If it is a hard rain, we know that it's a cleansing rain. When it hails, that's a purging rain. When we have meteors that bombard the earth we know that the universe is trying to provide us with additional insights that we did not have before. So we meditate on the meteor showers depending upon where they are and what the time frame is. The way we were told by the Creator is the Creator is bringing minerals from across the galaxy to the earth to provoke a different perspective on situations and we are evolving through that process.

We are called the Star Nation. We know that we have been on other planets before. There is a very old story that says all the other planets that are around the earth have been alive before and are now dead. And there has been existence on those planets but for one reason or another they have been extinct. We view the heavens, the constellations of stars, as part of what we call the logs of life. We view the stars and the planets as the archives of our past, present, and future. We know that when there is a birth, the essence of the spirit of that person travels great distances to get here. When reincarnation starts to happen and they chose a number of past lives to work on in this life they are anointed by the planets that are a part of the travel to this earth and that becomes their astrological chart. We know that when a child decides to be born it travels a path where different planets infuse that child with their natal chart. We also know that all the planets are very old spirits. They have decided to maintain the position and the personality and the essence of that planet. The stars are the maps of different locations of other galaxies. The Apache people use the constellation of Orion. We use Orion for our ceremonies because that's where we came from.

7
Stars

Aesculapius Ascends to the Stars (Greco-Roman)

Aesculapius was a wise and powerful healer. Being the son of Apollo and taught by the master teacher, Chiron, he was able to heal the sick no matter how close to death they were. In fact, with the aid of the goddess, Diana, he was even able to resurrect the dead. One day, Hippolytus, son of Theseus, was killed in a chariot accident. The kindhearted Aesculapius asked his dearest aunt, Diana Goddess of the Moon, to help him resurrect this poor lost soul. Diana lent her powers to those of Aesculapius and the youth once more lived. But down below, in Hades, the god of the Underworld, saw this act as a violation of the order of the Universe. Hades took his case to Zeus. Zeus knew what had to be done. He hurled a mighty thunderbolt at the healer, Aesculapius, killing him.

Apollo flew into a rage at this violation! He killed the Cyclops, the builders of the thunderbolt, out of revenge for his beloved son's death. Zeus punished his son, Apollo, for this outrage. He would become a servant to a king as a mortal. Stripped of his god powers for one year. Apollo served his penance. Aesculapius was missed by the people. They grieved for his death and they were saddened that no other would be able to heal as he did. Zeus, not being completely unreasonable, heard the cries of the people and the morning of his son. He took Aesculapius and placed him among the stars as the constellation, Ophiuchus. There, he would forever be known as the God of Healing.

When we gaze out into the sky on a clear night we see the magnificence of the stars. The constellations dance around the dark night evoking wonder and sparking feelings of magick. We see the same stars as did the people of, those long ago, ancient civilizations. Those stars have been soaring across our galaxy for billions of years. Many have been there since before the formation of the earth itself and will most likely be there after the earth is gone. We have all heard the words, "we are made out of stars". The chemicals that make up the heavens also make up our earth and our bodies. Not only are we connected with the stars through awe and wonder, we are connected with them by our flesh, blood, and bones.

Stars are born in nebulas. Stars like our Sun are formed when, diffuse hydrogen gas is contracted by gravity and becomes a protostar. The gravity of the protostar continues to contract and will start to spin very quickly and the center will heat up to over 10 million degrees. At this point the hydrogen of the star begins to burn off at such a high temperature that it will start to burn helium. This whole process will take 10 billion years. At which point, the star will become unstable and will cool and swell turning the star into a red giant. This is the birth, life, and eventual death of stars similar to our own.

As we know, stars emit an incredible amount of light and energy. If we could harness the energy of just one solar flare we would have enough energy to power a large city for many days. There are also many energies from stars we are just learning about. We observe the stars every night, but we are limited to what our human eye can see. We are able to see light in the colors in our spectrum of red, orange, yellow, green, blue, and violet. But there are many things we cannot see. Our human eyes cannot see infrared, the light "below" the color red. We also cannot see ultraviolet, the light that is "above" violet. Not until the 20th century were scientists able to discover more information about our universe. 1931 was the year that Karl Jansky first began to develop radio telescopes. It was not until 1970 that the Uhuru Satellite gave us a better view of our galaxy by observing x-rays. We also have discovered gamma rays and cosmic rays. Cosmic rays are fascinating to me because they are not really rays but are subatomic particles that are detected from deep in space. These energies or rays are recent findings in the hundreds of years that scientist have been observing our Universe. There maybe many more energies that are yet to be discovered. As shamans and magicians, we often hear that what was once considered magick is now considered science. There are many more subtle energies being emitted from the stars. These energies are astral-spiritual energies that we are able to use in magick.

Shamans, witches, and magicians have been observing the stars throughout human history. It was not until recently that we have had light pollution and the distraction of television that kept our attention away from the night sky. For thousands of years, humans have been gazing into the night and tracking the movement of the stars and planets. Sometimes the observation of the movement of the constellations told a story. In his book *Stars of the First People: Native American Star Myths and Constellations,* Dorcas S. Miller describes how the Micmac tribe observes the myth of the bear in Ursa Major (the big bear), "The narrative describes how the passage of the seasons on Earth is illustrated in the night sky. The bear (the bowl of the Big Dipper) emerges from its den (Northern Crown) in the springtime. Throughout the summer, seven hunters (stars in the handle of the Big Dipper and in Herdsman) pursue the bear across the northern horizon; one of the hunters (Mizar) carries a cooking pot (Alcor). The bear stands upright at this time. In the fall, several hunters drop out of the chase (these stars drop below the horizon for a few hours each night). The bear now lies on its back, preparing for hibernation. The remaining hunters kill the bear, whose spirit goes back to its den."

Native Americans often call themselves the People of the Star Nations. In many tribes, they believe that they were not created from the earth, but rather, they come from the stars. The Cherokee people believe that originally they lived in the Pleiades and were transplanted many thousands of years ago to the earth. In a similar fashion, the Apache people believe they are transplanted from the constellation of Orion.

The Egyptians believed that the physical plane was a mirror reflection of the Upperworld of the gods. They saw the Nile River as a direct reflection of the Milky Way. They also saw Egypt as the reflection of Osiris, himself, both physically and energetically. To begin with, let me orient you to the directions of Egypt. When we look at a map or globe we see that the Mediterranean Sea is North of Egypt. But to the view, according to the ancient Egyptians, the Mediterranean Sea is *under* Egypt. Therefore, we need to flip our maps of Egypt upside down to get a more accurate view of how the Egyptians view their land. Then land closest to the Mediterranean is Lower Egypt and the land near Sudan is Upper Egypt. The body of Osiris begins at his lower body or groin area at the Mediterranean Sea. So, there was a temple at Heliopolis to represent his sacral chakra. The following temples were built to be a mirror image of Osiris' chakras; Heliopolis (Sacral), Memphis, (Naval), Crocodopolis (Solar Plexus) and so on. It becomes very interesting to discover the temples that are built further up the Nile are representations of the chakras of Ra. Think of Ra, the creator God, as a spiritually higher octave or Osiris. So, the temple-chakras are those of Ra himself. These temple chakras are at Abydos (Sacral), Diospolis Parva (Naval), Dendera (Solar Plexus), Thebes (Heart), Esna (Throat), Edfu (Lower brow), Kom Ombos (Upper Brow), Philae Elephantine (Crown). The higher spiritual chakra was the temple of Abu Simbel.

The Egyptians also noticed that in Upper Egypt that the Nile curved around making the shape of Ursa Minor. Therefore, along with the idea that the temples were the chakras of Ra, they built them in the precise position that they would reflect the stars in Ursa Minor.

It is fascinating to me that the temples were also the spiritual training places of future priests. They would start at the lower chakra temples and end at the higher chakras. Each temple taught the candidates more spiritual techniques as the temple chakras got higher and would eventually lead to initiation into the priesthood. In his book *Land of the Fallen Star Gods: The Celestial Origins of Ancient Egypt*, J. S. Gordon says, "It would appear that main temples between Heliopolis and Abydos were therefore specifically designed to reflect definite zodiac associations. Consequently, by taking part in the particular rituals in each such temple, individual would automatically absorb an increasing degree of the nature of its particular God. The higher initiations were deemed to be influenced by both the zodiac and certain other constellations or stars - Ursa Major, Ursa Minor, Sirius, and Draco in particular."

Pyramids at Giza are of special importance to the story of the Egyptians. The three pyramids are in the precise position as the three stars (Alnitak, Alnilam, and Mintaka) in the belt of the Orion constellation. To the Egyptians, this constellation was a representation of Osiris himself. They also may have represented the energetic bodies of humans. That being the astral body, the mental body, and the spiritual body. But the pyramids at Giza had a more spiritual-magical importance than merely a representation. The air shafts located in the pyramid are directly aimed at the constellation of Orion and the stars Sirius, Kochab, and Alpha Draconis. Inside the pyramid it was a temple that had magical significance. The pyramid was believed to harness energies so that the candidate for the priesthood would be transformed by the powers of Osiris. Also, it was a magical battery for the dead to propel them into the Duat, the Underworld that was located in another dimensions in the stars which its entrance was in the constellation of Cancer.

In Britain, we have the mysterious burial mounds. These mounds served as the resting places for noble leaders and kings, but they also had a magical function. They may have been constructed with the similar intent as the Egyptian pyramids with the idea of the person buried would be sent to the Upperworld. Or perhaps they were used as a way to call upon the gods down for religious devotion. One of the most famous of the sacred mounds is Wayland's Smithy. This is a barrow located in Oxfordshire, Uffington. The barrows were believed to be constructed at the location at the rising stars of Aldebaran, Altair, and Alpha Crucis. There is a wonderful legend that the spirit of a smithy would shoe horses for travelers. The traveler would leave his horse and coins at the mound and he return with his horse properly shoed. There are many other mounds in Britain that were aligned with stars. The West Kennet Barrow are believed to be aligned to Sirius. The East Kennet Barrow seems to be aligned with Rigel. Unfortunately, the builders of these mounds and barrows left no written record so we have no way of knowing for sure the precise stars. We can only make an educated guess based on carbon dating of the mounds what star may have aligned with it.

Interestingly, near Wayland's Smithy is The Uffington White Horse. This is a pictograph of a horse that was cut into the earth. It looks white because of the chalk that lies underneath. This horse figure appears to be in alignment with the constellation of Taurus. More specifically, with the two stars Aldebaran and Gamma Tauri. In my opinion, if the figure was, indeed meant to be in alignment with Taurus, then perhaps this is more of a representation of a bull rather than a horse. On the other hand, we are assuming that these ancient peoples they saw a bull in the stars. Perhaps what they saw, instead, was a horse.

One form of Traditional Witchcraft is called Sabbatic Craft. This branch of witchcraft, made popular by the late Andrew Chumbley, focuses on stellar and celestial magick. Celestial magick in Traditional Witchcraft has many magical operations and techniques. One of them I find particularly interesting for the work of constellation magick; the invocation and joining with the stars of the constellation Draco for power and gnosis. In his book, *The Dragon Book of Essex,* Chumbley says, "Each of the fourteen points is a microcosmic facet of the Perfected Dragon-Body and is attributed to an anatomical division thereof, ranging from Tongue to the Tail. Each point functions as a nexus for corresponding energies and states of being, as a crossroads for the powers and the entities of the cosmos." What this means is that the energies of each of the stars of Draco has special corresponding powers that it gives to the witch. These powers include enchantment, mind control, power, gnosis, witch flight, and many others. The witch spends many enchanted nights of magical operation preparing for the joining of the stars to his or her body. Once done, the witch joins with the celestial body of Draco at the magically appointed time to obtain the powers.

In this branch of Traditional Craft, The Great Dragon is another form of The Devil, or the horned one Tubal Cain. The title of "Devil" does not mean Satan, but rather the horned one from pagan cosmology. Traditional Witchcraft is a combination of paganism, Judeo-Christian, and medieval magick and folklore. It was common for European witches to have what is called *dual faith.* This means that the common folk would sometimes keep their pagan beliefs along side with Christianity. So would refer to their pagan god of the horned one as The Devil, or Old Horny. If we look at more of the Christian side of Traditional Witchcraft we can see that in the lore, The Devil was Lucifer, the Angel of Light. At the same time, he was also referred to as "The Dragon". This is why in some depictions we see the Archangel Michael defeating The Great Dragon. Dragon has the double connotation of Lucifer and all of paganism combined. Michael was the destroyer of Paganism by defeating the dragon Lucifer. That being said, in Traditional Witchcraft, to conjure and join with Draco was to join with the Master of Witches, himself; the Horned One in Dragon form.

Of Stars and Gods

When we look up to the stars and allow our hearts to open and our mind to connect, we are able to see the gods within the stars. We can feel their presence and, if we are sensitive to the divine energies, we can feel their influence as well. The night sky is the home to the gods and they radiate their divine fires down to us. The stars are *not* the gods themselves, but a representation or a symbol of their eternal presence above our world. In modern patriarchal religions, their symbols include the crucifix, The Bible, The Koran, or other objects that we are able to hold. In shamanism, the symbols of the gods are the stars.

When shamans and priests observed the world around them, they saw that certain phenomenon corresponded with the rising and setting of stars. In Egypt, it was noticed that at certain times of the year when the star Sirius rises the Nile River flooded, giving the land the nutrient rich sediment of the river. These waters gave the land life and fertility. I can only guess that when the early Egyptian priests or shamans journeyed to Sirius they saw that this star was the goddess Isis. The shamans also noticed that when the sun was passing through certain constellations of the zodiac the seasons would change. Winter would give way to the life renewing powers of spring and later that year the warmth of summer would yield to the decaying fall as the constellations passed through the skies. Indeed, only the gods had this power and so it was that the stars themselves must be the gods.

Most of us know that the Greco-Romans saw the planets, or "wandering stars", as gods. This is where we get the names Mercury, Venus, Mars, Jupiter, and Saturn. The gods were, at times, also constellations. We have the god of healing, Asclepius, seen in the constellation of Ophiuchus as well has demi-gods such as Hercules and Castor and Pollux in the constellation of Gemini. The gods were ever present in pagan life and the luminaries that constantly moved through the night sky proved this to be so. When the Egyptians looked up into the night sky their gods watched over them. When Orion was in the sky, Osiris looked down up them. As did the goddess, Isis, when Sirius was bright. When the moon appeared, they saw Thoth. The darker gods, too, looked upon them; Set could be seen in Ursa Major and Nephthys known to be under the horizon. Our own star, the sun, could be several gods, depending upon its position in the sky. When the sun rose in the morning it was Horus. Horus dispelled the darkness of night (Set). At Midday the sun was the life giving Ra and at dusk was Atum. In India, the Hindus saw 27 gods in the night sky; there was Yama, the God of Death, in the stars of the dim triangle, Agni, the god of fire, in the Pleiades, and of course, Brahma the Creator of the Universe in Aldebaran as well as many others.

Star Magick

The use and exploration of the stars has been used in magick since the first humans saw the wonder and mystery of the luminaries above. Shamans, witches, and pagans know that tribal peoples were in tune with the environment around them. They heard the voices on the wind and the songs of trees, hills, and oceans. This was no different for the stars. Shamans recognized the energies emanating from the lights in the night sky. They felt its deeper magick and the effects they had upon the earth and beyond. Shamans spent many nights watching and tracking the movement of the stars each season each year. They paid close attention to how they affected people and the behaviors that were sometimes changed depending upon the phenomenon radiating from the night sky. Shamans journeyed to the stars and made allies with the spirits of deep space. Some were helpful and kind to humans. Some were not. The Shaman understood that earth is but one grain of sand in the vastness of the Universe. We have a unique perspective as humans, but as beings, we are not unique in the Universe. We are but one being in a sea of billions and perhaps trillions.

The shamans knew that humans are part of a much larger spiritual collective. There was much to be learned from the spirits and magick of the stars. If the lessons of the Underworld teaches us how to transcend our fears and connect with our ancestors then the lessons of the stars is to transcend our ego and connect with the spirits from above. Each star in each constellation has something to teach us. We can learn to become more powerful as living beings as well as learn to overcome our shortcomings. We can gain much wisdom from the spirits who are almost as old as the Universe itself. The perspective of the spirits of the stars are much different from the spirits of the earth. The stars are concerned with the "bigger picture" of the Universe, they have no interest in petty desires or even the basic needs of the individual. They care for the spiritual evolution of a species that will lead to the spiritual evolution of the Universe. As magical people, we have the ability to take the extraordinary powers of the stars and distill them to our human purposes. But the wise know that the stars have immeasurable power and to use it to elevate our consciousness and acquire power and gnosis of the cosmos.

Constellations and their magick

In the night sky, certain stars are brighter than others and, from our point of view on earth, the bright stars make patterns and pictographs for us to interpret. The ancient peoples such as the Egyptians, Babylonians, Hindus, and many other cultures watched the night sky and noticed it was telling a story. One of the most recognizable constellations in the night sky is Orion, the hunter. If we allow the night to tell us the story of Orion we see that his hunting dog, the constellation Canis Major is near him. We can also see that Orion is chasing lovely maidens that were transformed by Zeus into doves to escape him, the Pleiades. We can also see the Queen, Cassiopeia, who is sometimes upside down in the sky. This is because she was vain and offended the sea nymphs. The nymphs prayed to the gods to avenge the insult. So, the gods placed her in the sky and with the motion of the stars. Cassiopeia's punishment is seen when the constellation is sometimes forced upside down.

The constellations are seen as messengers from the gods. It is believed that astrology is how the gods speak with the people down on the earth below. Gavin White in his book, *Babylonian Star-Lore* says, "The constellations are best thought of as a part of a symbol system created by the gods by which they communicate their intentions to mankind." In this way, the gods let the people know what is to come, through astrology as well as give omens of their displeasure with humans. If the gods were not pleased with the offerings or the behavior of people it was thought that they would communicate this through the constellations. They would also herald certain phenomenon. The Greeks saw that when the constellation Hyades was in certain places in the night sky it was sure to bring the rainy season. When the "Dog Star" of Canis Major was seen in the summer months it was believed it was because of this bright star in conjunction with the sun that would bring the great heat. As we work with each constellation we will make allies with great spirits as well as progress on our spiritual path.

The Constellations

These are the constellations that we are accustomed to seeing in the Northern Hemisphere. I have given a brief description of each of the constellation. I highly encourage you to meditate and journey with each constellation and come up with your own interpretation of the energies. They may certainly resonate with those of the ancient people, but if you come up with something all your own, then all the better.

Orion

The hunter. In Greco-Roman myth, he is the hunter demi-god and lover of the goddess Diana. The Babylonian god Marduk. The Egyptian god Osiris. In both Arabic and Jewish astrology he is a Giant Man bound in heaven.

Ursa Major

Known as the Great Bear to Native Americans. The Egyptian monster Typhon. The Tower of Babel. In Greco-Roman myth it is Castillo, lover of Zeus, who was raised to the heavens after being transformed to a bear by Hera.

Draco

The Celestial Dragon. Sometimes referred to as the Upperworld Dragon. The dragon that guards the golden apples of the Greco-Roman gods. In Egypt it is Typhon the crocodile that tries to destroy Ra. The Nordic fire drake. The Master in some Traditional Witchcraft circles.

Andromeda

The Captive Princess. In myth, Andromeda was chained to a rock to await the dreaded sea monster. She awaits her hero to save her. The

galaxy of Andromeda is located here. The energies here ask
we bind ourselves to? Do we save ourselves or await ou
someone else comes along?

Ophiuchus

The serpent. Greco-Roman god of healing, Asclepius. In India, it is
Krishna standing on the head of a serpent. Placed midway between the
Poles. Balance of energies. In Greco-Roman myth, Aesculapius is the
balancer of life and death. He who gives life, but also gives death out
of mercy for the sick and wounded.

Cancer

The Crab. According to both the Egyptians and Babylonians, this is the
celestial gate way of the dead. Has a dimmer appearance than some
constellations and therefore seen at times to be a bad omen or herald ill
fortune. In China and India, it was seen as a flower.

Pleiades

In Native American star myths, it is the Seven Sisters. The Cherokee
believe that their people traveled to earth from this constellation. To
the Egyptians, the Pleiades represented the goddess Hathor. In Greco-
Roman star myth, these are the seven doves that carry ambrosia to the
gods. This constellation is seen as magical and brings the omens of the
mysteries of the Universe. Sometimes can be an omen of natural disaster.
Also represented the time of death during the month of November.

Perseus

The hero who saves Andromeda. Placed among the stars at his death.
He is seen as a hero-savor against evil beings or demons. Contains the

star, Algol. Algol is seen as Medusa's head, Lilith, and other demons.

Cygnus

The northern cross. Swan. In Greco-Roman myth, he is Orpheus, the musician. A magical bird of the stars. Sometimes seen as the Christian cross.

Cassiopeia

The Queen who was placed among the stars in humiliation for her vanity. This constellation was seen to contain the seeds of corn in preparation for planting.

Canis Major

The Great Dog. To the Egyptians, the star Sirius in this constellation represented the goddess Isis. Brings the life giving waters of the Nile River. In Greco-Roman myth, this is the hunting dog of Orion. Represents the blazing heat of summer. Thought to have power over the minds of canines.

Canis minor

One of Orion's hunting dogs. Is seen as Anubis, the Egyptian divine embalmer of the dead. One of Diana's hunting dogs. Energies resonate with the domesticated dogs.

Journeying to the constellations

When we journey to the constellations we will have a direct experience with the energies of the star group. We may learn more insights on the myths pertaining to them and meet other Upperworld spirits and perhaps other living beings. You may even find other entities that the ancient books do not speak of. My hope is that, along with ancient mythologies, you will use this technique to discover mythologies and stories on your own.

1. Decide which constellation you would like to work with. It should be a constellation that is overhead in the night sky. It is Okay if there is overcast on the night you wish to do your magick.

2. Look up at the constellation in the heavens. If there is overcast, visualize what the constellation will look like. Tune in to the magick and energy of the constellation. If you are inside, recreate the constellation using tea-lights. Gaze upon the candle constellation for at least 30 seconds so it leaves a visual imprint in your eyes. Then immediately look up to the ceiling. You should see the "spots" of the constellation projected on the ceiling.

3. Bring to mind any mythologies of the constellation. This will help you connect with the energies.

4. Astral project to the constellation. See the stars that make up the constellation in space, then see the character it represents. For example: For Orion, see the stars first, then visualize the divine hunter superimposed over the stars.

5. Introduce yourself as you would any new spirit you may meet. Ask any questions you may have or petition for magick.

6. Upon completion, give thanks to the spirit of the constellation and return to everyday waking consciousness.

Constellation Magick

This type of magick is akin to spirit summoning. We will be recreating the constellation on the ground, or table, as a magical conduit to summon the spirits of the constellation. Remember, that Upperworld spirits are more concerned with the bigger picture of creation and spiritual evolution of humans than day to day concerns. Before summoning constellation spirits, it may be helpful to speak with your gods and upperworld guide to help you understand the appropriate use of these spirits.

1. Decide on the constellation you would like to work with.

2. On the ground outside, or in your temple space, use tea lights to recreate the constellation. If you are outside, place the tea lights in a clear glass container such as a small mason jar. Glass jelly jars work well.

3. Look up into the night sky and find the constellation. If indoors, use the candle gazing technique from above. Tune in to the magick and energies of the constellation.

4. Using your own words, call upon the energy of the constellation down and superimpose it over the candle design of the constellation. For example, if you are using Orion see the divine warrior standing over the candles.

5. You may ask him questions or ask him to help you with magick. Spend some time in a light trance or meditation. Ask the spirit of the constellation what powers he or she may have and how you can use the in magick. You will be surprised all the magical abilities they will have that are not necessarily written in books.

Constellation Candle Magick

This type of magick is a powerful way to use the energies of the constellation to empower your spell craft. Stars have been used in magick for thousands of years. There are many spells that have been written to utilize the stars. This technique will help you use the constellations for your own magickal empowerment.

1. Decide on the constellation you would like to work with.

2. Use a colored candle that is synergistic to the magick at hand. If you are unsure, simply use a white candle.

3. Using a carving tool such as a blade, carve the constellation in your candle. Be sure to connect the lines to make the appropriate constellation character. Large candles work better for this, but do the best you can.

4. Go outdoors, if possible, and connect with the constellation. Visualize the power of the constellation coming down and empowering your candle.

5. Say whatever words that are appropriate to your spellcraft.

6. Light your candle and allow the magick to begin.

7. You may let your candle burn for 1, 3, 5 or , 7 nights. If you like, you can burn the candle on as many nights as there are stars in the constellation you are working with.

Astrology: The Procession of the Stars

There are many books on astrology and how to read and interpret the planets and the stars in your chart. My goal with this book is not to teach astrology, but to give you ideas and techniques, and hopefully, inspire you to come up with star magick on your own. Part of what I am doing with this current work is to use the stars and constellations as magical tools so that you can learn the wisdom, gnosis, and the powers of the stars. Western Astrology is but one option to do so. However, I do think it is important to keep in mind that the twelve zodiac signs can teach you a lot about our human condition, mental abilities, emotions, and spirituality.

In Vedic astrology, even though the stars and planets have the ability to predict the future, that is not there main concern. How the planets are arranged in your natal chart, not only helps you define characteristics of your personality, it helps you understand your karma that you need to address in this life. Vedic astrology teaches that before you incarnated in this life you waited until the planets were in the proper places, or houses, to best suit the karmic lessons you need to learn and evolve from. So, each planet is an opportunity to learn from its weaknesses and harness its strengths so you can live a happy balanced life.

The Zodiac should be seen as different aspects of our current incarnation upon this earth that we need to learn from. It is taught in western astrology that each soul must incarnate in each of the 12 zodiac signs to gain the wisdom and life experience of each sign. Each of the zodiac signs has something to teach. In the techniques below, I will teach you how to journey to the star portals of the constellations as well as speak with the spirits of each constellation. We will then learn to use the powers of the constellations in magick. Ideally, we should practice with all of the constellations that can be seen in the night sky in your area of the world. Feel free to begin with the constellation that you feel called to explore. You will want to journey to the constellations of the zodiac as well. By learning the lessons of the 12 zodiac signs, you will progress with your spiritual evolution more quickly. If you decide to work with the procession of the zodiac signs then you can begin with Aries and proceed in order until we end with Pisces. Otherwise, begin with your birth sign and progress through the zodiac. For example, if you are a Leo, begin with Leo and end with Cancer.

When working with the constellations, we want to journey to the

Upperworld to speak with the spirit of the constellation, then journey through the stars as a portal, and also call down the energies to use in magick in according the the nature of the constellation. It may help you to either draw or procure a picture of the constellation, as well as the zodiac symbol and set it before you with candles and incense that is appropriate to the work at hand. When choosing an incense, use a scent that corresponds the ruling planet. Otherwise, you can use sage, sandalwood, or frankincense. You can also use the constellation candle magick technique to incorporate the lessons of each zodiac sign in your life.

Aries

Key word: I Am.

March 21-April 20. Ruled by Mars.

Cultivate kindling the internal flame and build self-confidence. Learn to use the spark of energy to propel you forward in projects.

Learn to understand arrogance and bullying. Learn to use your energies wisely.

Taurus

Key word: I Have.

April 21-May 20. Ruled by Venus.

Cultivate the steadiness of right action and personal values. Learn to be patient with others. Have a healthy understanding of the financial world and possessions.

Learn to understand loss and what it means to be free of attachment. Understand self worth.

Gemini

Key word: I Think.

May 21-June 20. Ruled by Mercury.

Cultivate the power to harmonize opposing forces. Understand the power of communication and logic. Be aware of the power of versatility. Learn to control the powers of the mind. Be of service to others.

Cancer

Key Word: I Feel.

June 21-July 20. Ruled by the Moon.

Cultivate the ability to nurture others. Understand and learn about your psychic abilities. Empower your empathic abilities.

Learn to control your emotions and be aware of the feelings of others.

Leo

Key word: I Will.

July 21-August 20. Ruled by the Sun.

Cultivate courage to go forward on your spiritual path and nurture loyalty to friends and family. Understand what it is to be honest and have integrity.

Learn to have discipline with your action and behaviors and give up any need to control others.

Virgo

Keyword: I Analyze.

August 21-Sept 20. Ruled by Mercury.

Cultivate the evolution of mind, body, and spirit. Understand the value of humility and patience.

Learn to see the beauty and perfection in all things and find inner strength.

Libra

Keyword: I Balance.

Sept 21-October 20. Ruled by Venus.

Cultivate the energies of companionship and the union of the self and spirit. Understand the function of balance in the universe. Be aware of the need of diplomacy.

Learn to understand when to sacrifice for others and when to stay strong in your convictions.

Scorpio

Keyword: I Create.

Oct 21-November 20. Ruled by Pluto.

Cultivate the energies of transformation. Learn how to transcend the ego so that you may understand the magick of the spirit. Allow sensual pleasures to teach your consciousness to ascend to the bliss of the gods. Learn to have compassion for those who do not understand the ways of spirit.

Sagittarius

Key word: I Perceive.

November 21-December 20. Ruled by Jupiter.

Cultivate your understanding of emotions and thoughts of others. Allow the freedom of new journeys to inspire your passions.

Learn to create a peaceful environment for all concerned. Become aware of the discipline needed to spiritual growth.

Capricorn

Key word: I Use.

December 21-January 20. Ruled by Saturn.

Cultivate your higher sense of purpose and destiny upon the earth. Allow your leadership abilities to grow. Become mindful of the influence of power and financial gain.

Learn to have compassion and love for those who are less spiritually evolved and teach them to the best of your abilities.

Aquarius

Key word: I Know.

January 21-February 20. Ruled by Uranus.

Cultivate your leadership abilities and your idealism for a better world. Allow the rebirth of spirit to transform your consciousness and your soul.

Learn to understand that which binds you and keeps you from going forward on your spiritual journey.

Pisces

Keyword: I Believe.

February 21-March 20. Ruled by Neptune.

Cultivate your spiritual calling and embrace your psychic nature; this is the path to Universal consciousness. Allow yourself to have both your physical desires as well as the union with spirit.

Learn to see the light, as well as the darkness, within yourself as whole and complete.

Star Portals

One of my favorite Upperworld magicks is to work with star portals. Star portals are created when the energies of stars criss-cross each other creating a celestial vortex. This is similar to a wormhole. The difference between a wormhole and a star portal is that a wormhole will take you to different parts of the Galaxy in the physical plane. Also a wormhole, theoretically, is not constant and you may not always know where you end up. A star portal is a set portal to a different astral dimension. When you discover a star portal, you will always be taken to the same place. Star portals are not always a gateway to celestial spirits, they may be able to take you to different dimensions in the far reaches of the Universe.

The easiest way to find a star portal is through the constellations themselves. Each zodiac as well as all constellations can help you find celestial spirits. In my circle, we used the constellation of Draco as a star portal. We found that when we journeyed through the portal, we found a dimension that was home to spiritually advanced beings. They had magnificent temples and a hierarchy of priests and leaders. Because they were spirits of advanced star magick, they were not interested with working with anyone who was not serious about star magick and advanced Upperworld workings.

Another way to work with star portals is through the interconnection between constellations. Yes, not only do the constellations themselves become a gateway to different realities but so do the in between spaces between them and all other stars. I highly encourage you to experiment with this sort journeying and magick. This is where advanced shamanism and magick happen. I have not seen many books on this subject and there are few people who do this type of work. Instead of relying on other shamans and magicians to teach you what to do, you must discover the magick for yourself. How wonderfully exciting this is. You are truly becoming an innovative magician with this work!

To Journey through the the Star Portals

1. Decide which constellation you would like to work with. It should be a constellation that is overhead in the night sky. It is Okay if

there is overcast on the night you wish to do your magick.

2. Look up at the constellation in the heavens. If there is overcast, visualize what the constellation will look like. Tune in to the magick and energy of the constellation. If you are inside, recreate the constellation using tea-lights. Gaze upon the candle constellation for at least 30 seconds so it leaves a visual imprint in your eyes. Then immediately look up to the ceiling. You should see the "spots" of the constellation projected on the ceiling.

3. Astral project yourself to outer space until you find yourself in front of the constellation.

4. Know that the constellation is a gateway to another dimension. See the stars connecting to each other forming the constellation you have chosen.

5. Project through the star portal.

6. Take notice of where you are. What does the sky and ground look like? What is the landscape? Are there beings there? What do they look like?

7. Always remember that you are a visitor to these places and you must have the courtesy of a foreign traveler. Be respectful.

8. When you are ready, come back the way you came. And come back to everyday waking consciousness.

9. Journal your experiences.

The Planets

The planets dance nightly through the heavens above. They weave through the constellations and shine brightly in their power. They are magnificent and beautiful hovering in the night sky as they teach us about ourselves and the world around us through their energies. The word "planet" means *wanderer*. To the ancient observers of the skies, the planets were the stars that moved freely about as the stars in the constellations seems "fixed" in their positions. Each planet seemed to have its own power and its own majestic attributes. They noticed when the planets were in specific places in the sky it had an impact on the emotions, thoughts, behaviors, and deeds of the people. There was magick emanating from these wanderers.

Cultures such as the Greeks, Egyptians, and Babylonians saw them either as gods or symbols of the gods. Each planet had its own divine powers that affect man and the energies of the earth. The planets have inspired poetry, stories, and myths such as this Homeric Hymn.

"Mighty Ares, gold-helmed chariot master,
shield bearer, bronze-armored city guard, strong willed,
strong armed, untiring spear strength, defence of Olympus,
father of Victory in war, aid to Themis,
tyrant to enemies, leader of righteous men,
wielding manhood's scepter, your red orb whirling
among the seven paths of the planets through the ether
where your fiery stallions bear you above the third orbit..."
-Homeric Hymn, translated by Diane J. Rayer

Luna - The Moon

"It is in fact likely that the fundamental notion of a life-structuring relationship between the heavenly world and that

of man was derived from the realization, both in experience and in thought, of the force of the lunar cycle."
-Joseph Campbell *Primitive Mythology*

Diana and Endymion (Greco-Roman)

There was a shepherd named Endymion. Night after night, as he watched his sheep, he would gaze up at the moon and dream of the goddess, Diana. His love for her could be felt throughout space and time. Diana took notice of this handsome shepherd and smiled back at him as he looked dreamy eyed at her. One night, as he slept, she appeared to him and gave him a kiss then returned to the heavens.

Diana grew to adore the sweet gaze of her shepherd as she passed him by in the night sky. Each night, when he slept, she gave him a kiss. Then one night, before she reached his hill, where he would watch her, Diana heard a loud scream come from Endymion. In a flash of light, she appeared before Endymion. He lie gravely wounded from the bites of wolves. He was protecting his sheep from the predators. His wounds were too deep for her to heal him. She knew her beloved shepherd would soon pass through the gates of Hades.

"I do not fear death," Endymion said. "I fear never again your nightly kiss."

Diana had to act fast. With her magick, she cast a spell upon him that he would forever sleep and never awaken to be taken into death.

So now to this very day, before Diana, the moon, takes her nightly journey across the sky, she steps into her sleeping chamber where her beautiful shepherd forever sleeps and gives him a kiss. As she peeks into his dreams, she sees that he forever dreams...of her.

We do not know exactly what the origin of our moon is. There are a couple of theories that scientist have. The first is that the earth and moon were formed around the same time as the rest of our solar system and the earth's gravity caught the moon and kept it in its gravitational field. The second theory is that during the formation of our solar system, a large body struck the earth knocking a portion off of it and the earth's gravitational field kept the chunk of earth from escaping out into the universe. The moon is about a quarter the size of earth and has a diameter of 2,159 miles. It is approximately 238,900 miles away and has a rotation of 28-29 days around the earth. The moon governs the tides of the ocean and also the waters of animals and humans who live on the earth. As the moon rotates around the earth, the gravitational tug of the moon causes the tides to change.

The moon is one of the most primal symbols and powers known to us. She captures our imaginations and that part of our animal psyche that wishes to escape into the bliss of the night. It was believed in Victorian times that people caught outside under the full moon may go insane. This is the root of the word "Lunacy". My grandfather was a mortician and he would say that on the night of the full moon many more bodies came in than usual. Most people do not realize the power the moon holds over us. Perhaps it is simply her gravitational pull, but I believe Lady Luna has a powerful magick that is all her own. She is honored by witches, magicians, and shamans alike and she is powerful and beautiful. We know that when the moon is full that is the most powerful time to do magick. We also know that when the moon is dark that is a wonderful time to banish, curse, and use the magick of luna for a darker, primal purpose.

The full moon is a powerful time for ghosts, spirits, and nature spirits to be seen. The moon's rays have ionized particles in the air that helps us see the astral bodies of the spirits. It is also a time for shamans and were-people to shape-shift into animals and howl to the Queen of the night sky. If we look at The Moon card of the tarot we see a domesticated dog and wolf howling at the moon. It is the power of the moon that sparks the primal side of all nature to become in tune with their primal aspect. No one can escape it. No matter how "civilized" one may think they are. The Moon governs the sea and has powers over the ocean and emotions.

As the powers of Sol govern the everyday waking consciousness so does Luna govern the subconscious. She is the power of night and of magick. The moon teaches us how to expand our psychic powers and connect to the astral plane. She is also the planet most connected with illusions or untruths. Under the magick of the moon things take on a dreamy romantic quality. This is also the realm of dreams and fantasies.

The Moon
rules our emotions. The subconscious. Cycles. Illusions. Magick. Witchcraft. Psychic Powers. Dreams. Purification. The Astral Plane.

Color: Violet

Number: 9

Herbs: Coconut, Eucalyptus, Gardenia, Jasmine, Lavender, Lemon, Moonwort

Stones: Aquamarine, Amethyst, Beryl, Moonstone, Quartz Crystal, Pearl, Selenite

Metal: Silver

Day: Monday

Spirit: Phul

Sephiroth: Yesod

Mercury

Coyote Steals Sun's Tobacco (Apache)

One day, Coyote went to visit his cousin, Sun. Sun was not home but he noticed the bag of tobacco hanging on the wall. He asked Sun's wife to give him some tobacco to smoke while he waits for sun. Time went on and Sun had not come home. Without Sun's wife knowing, Coyote took more tobacco and placed it in his own bag. He then said, "Sun is taking too long to get home so I will go home now." Coyote went on his way. When Sun got home he saw that his tobacco was gone and his wife told him about Coyote. He began chasing Coyote, but Coyote was very fast. As Coyote ran, tobacco seeds fell out of his sack and began to grow the first tobacco plants.

When Coyote got back to his people they asked him to share the tobacco, but Coyote was greedy and said no. So the people devised a plan. They would trick Coyote into a pretend marriage. They dressed a boy as a girl and pretended to give him a wife. Coyote gave his new pretend wife his tobacco as a wedding gift and the "wife" then gave it to the people. But, Coyote discovered that his wife was, indeed, a boy! Coyote sent the pretend wife back to the people and demanded his tobacco to be returned. The people laughed and said no! And this is how the sacred tobacco came to the Apache people.

Mercury is the planet that is closest to the sun. From our point of view here on earth, he can only be seen near the sun. His diameter is only 3,030 miles across and is very small with relation to the earth. The rotation around the sun is 88 earth days, but his mercurial day is 58 days. So one day on mercury is one third of its year. That leads to very extreme temperatures on both sides of the planet. The day side can reach above 127 degrees Celsius and the night side can go as low as -183 degrees Celsius. This is seemingly "bipolar" temperature difference is interesting to me because if we look at one of the constellations Mercury rules is Gemini. Gemini left unbalanced has a tendency to flit back and forth from one extreme mood to another. Mercury is riddled with craters and has no atmosphere. It does, however, have a magnetic field that helps deflect some of the solar winds. It also has a very dense core believed to be made of iron.

Mercury is the god of swiftness and travel. When we observe Mercury in the heavens he wisps back and forth very quickly in the skies. He also governs logic and reason. He is the planet of scientist and alchemist. He is not concerned with fantasy or romance only the cold hard truths. To him it is not about judgement, but about finding out the hows and the whys. Mercury can teach us about the spoken and written word. In magick, to write down your spells has a very powerful effect. Once written, than spoken aloud, the energies of Mercury travel very quickly throughout the ethers. The god Mercury-Hermes is a trickster spirit. Like Coyote in the myth above, trickster gods tend to "mess things up" in order for the people to get the things they need.

When Mercury goes into retrograde we panic. We have a fear that everything in our lives will go haywire or break. We just know traffic will be awful and emails will get lost. The Native American people know Mercury in retrograde to be an opportunity for spiritual growth. For Native American Peoples, this is a time to deal with unresolved Karma. The Universe does not like a buildup of energy. This is the time to address those actions, behaviors, and things from the past that we have been putting off to the side. Mercury in retrograde makes us deal with our baggage if we want to or not. Hopefully, at the end of it we have cleared our energies so that better opportunities of growth and healing can occur. It is interesting to note that people whose Mercury was in retrograde upon the time of birth have an easier time with this.

Mercury rules

Logic. The intellect. Communication. Travel. Contracts and

agreements. Technical skills. Computers and technology. Journeys.

Color: Orange

Number: 8

Herbs: Caraway, Clover, Dill, Fennel, Fern, Flax, Lemongrass, Peppermint

Stones: Agate, Aventurine, Citrine, Jasper, Topaz, Turquoise

Metal: Mercury

Day: Wednesday

Spirit: Ophiel

Sephiroth: Hod

Venus

Ezili Freda (Haitian Vodou)

I come to the dance in my finery
This beautiful woman whom I use as my "horse"
She is fitting for a goddess such as me
But she could use a little make up
I shall pretty her face to show my splendor
There are many beautiful men here
No, my husbands will not mind
No man can own my desire
 For desire cannot be contained
I kiss them with passion
and they are spellbound with my beauty
For my faithful followers
I will give love, wealth, and luck
And in return I expect full adoration

They will adore me and I will gift them their desires

It is my heart and soul that yearns for great love

Do I not deserve all your love?

Am I not the goddess of your dreams?

I will be yours and you will be mine

Alas, the dance is coming to an end

Please, do not go

Accept my love, do not go

Why must love end in tears?

Tears of love are the most terrible

Remember me in your heart

For desire is the beginning of love

Venus is the second planet in our solar system and is considered earth's sister planet. She has a similar size to Earth and is the brightest planet seen in earth's sky. Her rotation around the sun is 225 days and each venusian day is 243 earth days. This means that a year on Venus is shorter than one of her days. Interestingly, she rotates in the opposite direction of earth. She spins east to west where the earth spins west to east. She has a very thick cloud coverage in her atmosphere that is made mostly of carbon dioxide but does not have many storms. She does have acid rain from time to time. Venus' surface is mostly rocky plains with a few mountains here and there. Her surface has many active volcanoes and there are sometimes lava rivers that flow through her terrain.

Venus has always had a special place in our hearts throughout history. Venus is known as the morning and evening star. In some cultures she was seen as the goddess of love and yet in others this planet was thought to be Lucifer himself in the night sky because of its brightness. Lucifer, after all, is the light bearer. Venus is considered our sister planet because of her close proximity and her closeness in size to our earth. In the past, we fantasized about beautiful women aliens who inhabited that world who wish to fulfill the desires of men. We daydreamed that she had vast oceans and cities like ours. Unfortunately, as wonderful of a story this is, it simply is not the case. The energies of love and devotion will always be felt as we watch her in the evening and morning sky.

Venus is the goddess of love and sensuality. She teaches us how to open our hearts and allow people to see the "real" us. She also teaches us how to care for others with an open heart. When our hearts are broken, Venus is the planet that can help us learn from it and grow. She also governs art and beauty. She shows us that what is repulsive to others may be beautiful to us. Venus is also the planet of sexuality. It is through her longing for union do we understand the equilibrium of opposites. We have all heard the saying "opposites attract". It is through this that we challenge ourselves to be more than we are today and spiritually and emotionally grow. Our capacity to love is greater than we think and Venus is very happy to challenge us to love others as well as ourselves. Venus also is the attainment of Nirvana through ecstatic dance and songs that lead you to a state of bliss.

The Rose is one of the sacred flowers of Venus. It is the sensual softness of the petals and the life color or red. Like love itself, the beauty of the flower is tempered by the thorns. We have all bled for love in one way or another. We have had a broken heart or bled during the pain of childbirth. We have sacrificed ourselves so that we may be sacrificed to our desires to be joined with another. Yet it is through union that we learn to be more ourselves, so long as our beloved is supporting our development and we theirs.

Venus rules

Love. Honor. Friendship. Romance. Sexuality. Female Mysteries.

Art. Luxury.

Color: Green

Number: 7

Herbs: Burdock, Cardamom, Catnip, Foxglove, Geranium, Hibiscus, Hyacinth, Rose

Stones: Cat's Eye, Coral, Emerald, Malachite, Pink Calcite, Rose Quartz

Metal: Copper

Day: Friday

Spirit: Hagith

Sephiroth: Netzech

Sol - The Sun

The Return of Balder (A Modern Norse Tale)

I sit at the mighty tables

Deep inside the halls of Hel, the Underworld

The winter of my life

From above, I hear the chaos of war

I know that the end of all things is near

The halls of Hel are being prepared for permanent guests

I have never seen such preparations

All that was once wonderful on earth

The land, sea, sky, and stars are all gone-they are gone

All sides of the war have lost

The magick of Hel has waned and the bonds that keep me here

Are no more

I am able to leave this solemn place and return to the worlds above

But all is lost

My father and brothers are dead, but some still live

Vidar, Vali, Magni, Modi, still live

From the sacrifice of their lives

My life and vigor return to me

Like the growing warmth of Spring

My powers of light and illumination are returned to me

I use my magick to save and heal those last two humans who remain

Hidden in the trunk of mighty Yggdrasil

The woman, named Life and the man, Life's Yearning

I use my shining light to help the earth heal from the terror of war

Together with Vidar, Vali, Magni, Modi

We rebuild the heavens and return the stars to the sky

A new age, the Summer of life

Will we do things better this time

Or will we start it all again, only to be destroyed?

And the cycles of the Universe continue forth.

The Sun is our home star and the source of all life in our solar system. He has a diameter of 865,000 miles. The surface of the sun has a temperature of 5500 degrees Celsius. The sun does spin but because it is not a solid structure is spins in a very unique way. The surface near the poles spin every 34 earth days, while the surface at the equator spin every 25 earth days. While the planets rotate around the sun, so does the sun rotate around the Milky Way Galaxy. This take about 225 million years to complete the great cosmic year. The Sun is primarily made of Hydrogen with the remaining being Helium. It is the combustion of these gases at the core of the sun which makes the energy and light of the sun. The sun emits what is called *solar wind*. Solar wind is charged particles being sent out from the sun constantly. When solar winds hit the earth's magnetic field the aurora borealis is the result.

The sun has been worshiped and honored throughout the history of human civilization. He is the life bringing and is a symbol of the male mysteries in many pagan cultures such as the Egyptians and Native Americans. The golden rays bring warmth and vitality to the earth. The sun is very powerful in magick and its powers can be used for many things. The movement of the sun in our sky heralds the seasons and we watch his journey so that we may know when winter is coming and when the daylight hours are returning so that we may plant our crops in the spring.

Stonehenge

Stonehenge was built approximately 3000 BCE. No one knows exactly why the stone circle was built, but there are very good educated guesses that say that it was built for religious and magical purposes relating to the setting of the Midwinter sun. There have been many archaeologists and astronomers who have tried (and hoped) to figure out if the great stones, called *trilithons,* were built like a star clock, similar to the pyramids of ancient Egypt. The configuration of the stones could calculate the rising and settings of stars only with a vivid imagination. The primary astrological calculation was, indeed, the death of the Midwinter sun. This is very plausible because this signified the end of the solar year and the beginning of the new solar year. This also marked the beginning of winter and the long cold months ahead. Stonehenge had a purpose of honoring the magick of the sun and welcoming winter as well as preparing the community for trials to come at the dark time of year.

Unfortunately, all the reasoning the Neolithic people had for creating such a grand temple would be lost to the magick of time.

Lakota Sundance

The Lakota Sundance is a sacred ceremony performed during the summer months that ask the creator, Wonka Tonka, for a vision or a sacred prayer to aid the people or someone who they love. The Sundance is a community ceremony that involves the dancers, drummers, medicine men, and those who support the dancers. Those who dance the sun dance are taught sacred Sundance songs and spend many days before praying and performing the *inipi*, the sweat lodge. When the day comes to dance, they are prepared in a sacred way. Then, two little metal spikes are pierced through the skin of their chest that is attached to a cord that is attached to a central pole. The dancers dance and sing their sacred songs until spirit overtakes them and they fall back with the spikes ripping through the skin. It is then the creator gives them sacred messages and visions.

The Sun helps us understand who we truly are. He teaches us to tap into our higher consciousness and that of our Holy Guardian Angel, who I believe, is our higher self personified. The Sun's heat and light are very healing to the earth and all living things. He's the warmth of spring that heats up the land from the coldness of winter. Sun gods are sometimes seen as healing gods. They are prayed to and given offerings so that they may bestow their powers of regeneration and balance to the people. The Sun's brightness and vitality attracts success. Success is different to everyone. Jupiter's powers are those of jobs and money, but The Sun's powers are those of success in any endeavour. The writer is published, the actor gets a movie roll, the student gets into college, the poet gets an audience. Whatever success means to you that is what you shall receive. Understand, though, the success you receive will propel you forward spiritually and money is not the prime goal with the Sun. Where the Moon is the illusion of night, the Sun is the truth and understanding of the day. Everything is now seen for what it is and all of its flaws. What once was fantasized now is reality. The Sun reminds us to be careful what we wish for.

The Sun rules

Healing, Music, Success, Balance, Spirituality, Higher Self, Obtaining Goals, Holy Guardian Angel

Color: Yellow

Number: 6

Herbs: Bay, Chamomile, Copal, Frankincense, Juniper, Orange, Rowan, Rue, Sunflower

Stones: Amber, Carnelian, Pyrite, Sunstone, Tiger's Eye, Yellow Calcite

Metal: Gold

Day: Sunday

Spirit: Och

Sephiroth: Tiphereth

Mars

The Wrath of Sekhmet (Egyptian)

It came to pass that the creation of Ra, humanity, began to become rebellious. They hurt each other and no longer worshiped the gods. Their hearts grew dark and cold and they began to turn on each other. The gods held council and asked the wise Ra what they should do. Wise Ra had the gift of foresight. He saw only destruction and death. There was only one thing to do, destroy humanity.

Ra sent the powerful goddess, Sekhmet, down to earth to destroy humanity. The great Lioness goddess bolted down with a most terrible roar! In one day, she slaughtered thousands of people. The world shall be purified of evil! All that remained was blood and death. Ra saw his creation almost destroyed. In a change of heart, gracious Ra took pity on the human race and decided they had suffered enough and they should live. But, Sekhmet became bloodthirsty and was planning another slaughter the next day.

Quickly, Ra sent for a red mineral that would color beer to look as though it were blood. He poured the blood looking beer all over Egypt. When Sekhmet saw what she thought was blood, she drank more than her fill. She became intoxicated and was easily subdued. Ra took the drunk Sekhmet back to the heavens and saved humanity from Sekhmet's wrath. Ra, the merciful one, saved us all from the battle rage of Sekhmet.

Mars is the fourth planet in our solar system. Mars is much smaller than the earth and has a red rocky surface. He travels around the sun in 687 days and one Martian day is equal to roughly 24 earth hours. The average temperature on Mars is -23 Celsius. He has an axial tilt similar to earth and therefore has four seasons just as Earth does. Mars has a thin atmosphere and can have clouds and dust storms. One of the more prominent features are the ice caps at the polls that are made of carbon dioxide. The surface of mars contains rocky plains, mountains, valleys, channels, and volcanoes.

Mars has been the subject of debate for many years. It was believed that there was life on Mars and they may be a technically advanced civilization. It was believed that the channel like structures seen on the surface of Mars may have been made by some kind of life form. H.B.

Wells, author of *War of the Worlds*, told the story of invaders from Mars who wished to destroy humans and take over the earth. When it was played on the radio in 1938 it is believed that people panicked at the thought of an actual invasion. There have been many other books and movies about Martian invaders. There is even a DC Comics superhero named Martian Manhunter. Who has been recently featured on the TV show *Supergirl*. Recent space expeditions to Mars has found no evidence of a Martian civilizations. However, there are some people who believe that Mars was once a thriving world that has died out from natural and industrial disaster. What we do know is that Mars' inner core was once hot and active but has gone cold.

Mars is the planet of courage, strength, and aggression. Without the fires of Mars we would be stagnant and lethargic. He is also the remover of obstacles. There are many times in our lives that things get in the way of our desires and our spiritual progress. Some of those things we may have put there ourselves without realizing it. Mars can help you destroy energetic blocks that are holding back your evolution. One of the sayings of Mars is, "Now is the time! I am not waiting anymore to change my life!" Mars kindles the fires in us that make us want to fight for what is right and protect our loved ones. Mars is also the passion of love. Not the sensual love of Venus, but the primal desire to mate with another and give our fires to another. The Greco-Roman God, Mars, is the god of war. There are many reasons countries go to war. Some crave power, some religious dominance, but the true warrior protects those who cannot protect themselves. He or she finds the virtue and honor for standing up for what is right prepared to sacrifice their liberties, freedoms, and even their lives.

Mars rules

Male Sexuality, Warrior, Energy, Taking Action, Aggression,

Personal Will, Divine Will, Battle/ War

Color: Red

Number: 5

Herbs: Basil, Coriander, Dragon's Blood, Garlic, (All) Peppers, Tobacco, Wormwood

Stones: Bloodstone, Garnet, Obsidian, Pipestone, Red Jasper, Ruby,

Metal: Iron

Day: Tuesday

Spirit: Phalegh

Sephiroth: Geburah

Jupiter

Quetzalcoatl Blesses the People (Aztec)
I am winged serpent of the heavens
Born from the womb of the Star Goddess
Ruler of the sky world and earth world
For I am god and yet human king of the Aztecs
I see all those beings who walk beneath the starry skies
It is I who taught humans who to plant corn
Stolen from the gods themselves
It is I who taught the people smithcraft
To create tools and jewelry
It is I who is called upon to temper the ore of spirit
Into something more precious
And it is I who said human sacrifice should be no more

For this, I have made enemies from the gods

They say this is weakness

But It is my love for the people and all creation

That no one should die an unnecessary death

For this I may be sacrificed

To the gods and to myself

So the people can be transformed anew

I rule for the people, and the gods

I am the balance of the ethereal heavens

And the rocky earth below

The fifth planet in our solar system is Jupiter. Jupiter is known as a gas giant and is the second brightest planet seen in Earth's sky. His diameter is over 11x greater than that of the earth. His rotation around the sun is nearly 12 Earth years, however, the Jovian day is only about 10 earth hours. Jupiter's core is surrounded by liquid hydrogen. Above this is liquid molecular hydrogen and then there is the thick atmosphere. Jupiter's atmosphere has what is called "cloud belts". These are the belt like features that constantly spin around the atmosphere. One of his most prominent features is the great red spot located in the southern hemisphere. This red spot is one of Jupiter's great storms. There are many other storm spots as well. Jupiter emits very strong radio waves and has super strength radiation in its atmosphere. Jupiter is one of earth's protectors. The gravitational force of Jupiter attracts asteroids to plunge down to its surface keeping them far away from earth.

Jupiter is seen as the King of the gods. His brightness is seen vividly in the night sky. When it is hazy out and you cannot see the stars, you can see Jupiter. Jupiter was thought to be a "failed star". Some scientist believed that when our solar system was forming that Jupiter was intended to be a star but for reasons unknown never took the process of becoming a star. We know now that this is not the case. Jupiter's energies are those of expansiveness. His energies are moving ever forward in all directions. His direction is that for the betterment of the self and of the evolution of the Universe. He is also the ruler of the heavens and can help us in "ruling" our own lives. Jupiter has the power to bring us monetary gain. The King cannot rule the kingdom without the gold coin. He must pay for his army the well-being of the kingdom. It is with his powers can you obtain the job of your dreams. Or at least, the job that will pay your rent until you find the job of your dreams.

Jupiter is the planet of order. The energies here must have an ebb and flow so that the correct cycles can go forth. For the solar system and the Universe to sustain life, it must have an order. Gravity must be in place to keep the planets spinning around the sun. There must be light and warmth to sustain life. The elements of gas, heat, liquid, and solid, but be in the correct place for the universe to function; especially for the function of our planet earth to sustain life.

Jupiter Rules
Order, Leadership, Jobs, Money, Responsibility, Promotions, Peace, Diplomacy

Color: Blue

Number: 4

Herbs: Anise, Dandelion, Hyssop, Linden, Liverwort, Nutmeg, Sage, Star Anise

Stones: Lapis Lazuli, Lepidolite, Jade, Rhodochrosite, Sapphire, Sodalite

Metal: Tin, Aluminum

Day: Thursday

Spirit: Bethor

Sephiroth: Chesed

Saturn

The Bliss of Kali Ma (Hindu)

I come from the bliss of darkness

Created from the despair of the gods

Fearful of demons taking over the heavens

But I am the bliss of darkness

The bliss of destruction; I know only the wonder of chaos

It is through my sacred voice

The Universe was created with my beloved Shiva

Shiva, he who creates and I who destroy

Together we are the Universe: The ebb and flow of totality

I stand on his body, not out of victory of triumph

But of love of infinite possibility

I am the bliss of darkness

I am she who brings the lessons of Karma

To fearful men who know no bliss

I am the destruction of Time

All things must return to me to be reformed into new Universes

I am she who forces you to let go

Of all things you once loved

 So you may return to my darkness of rebirth

For pain, sorrow, tears, and heartbreak are my gifts

So that you may experience a spiritual life

and through me, discover

The bliss of my darkness

Saturn is our sixth plant and is another gas Giant and is only second to Jupiter. It is famous for its spectacular rings. It travels around the sun in 29 years and its day is equal to 10 hours and 14 minutes. Saturn's surface is made up of liquid hydrogen and helium and her core is metallic. She has a density that is less than water. Much of the energy that comes from Saturn is from the core as well as a very strong gravitational pull. Both Saturn and Jupiter emit heat and energy. Saturn has three main ring systems which are made of debris and water that has turned to ice. The rings have a diameter of 169,000 miles but are very thin. At times, Saturn can be one of the brightest bodies in the night sky.

Saturn is the planet of constriction. In Greco-Roman mythology, Saturn-Kronos, is the father of Zeus-Jupiter, Hera-Juno, and several others. He heard a prophecy that stated his sons would over through his rulership. To prevent this, he swallowed his children. The energies of Saturn are of the old ways that refuse to give way to the new. As shamans and pagans, we are reclaiming our old traditions of the earth, but we must remember to leave out those old traditions that are not suited for the 21st Century. We must honor the old but create the new. Saturn is also the planet of death. In the ancient world, Saturn was the last observable planet. Because of this he ruled the time of death and decay. In Rome, they celebrated a festival that marked the winter known as Saturnalia. This is when Lords became peasants and peasants became Lords. This showed the topsy-turvy time of winter and the dark strange energies of Saturn. Because Saturn ruled death, he also ruled the earth and all elements under it such as metals and stones.

Saturn is also known as the great destroyer. The god Saturn carries a scythe reaping all things that have outlived its usefulness. Where Mars removes blocks and gets things moving, Saturn destroys the old to make way for the new. He also removes the sick and those things that cannot be repaired. In the great machine that is the Universe, when a sprocket is broken beyond repair, Saturn removes it so a new one can take its place. There is no judgment to the old sprocket. It is about the efficiency of the machine.

Saturn is used to show us our limitations and what is keeping us from succeeding. The constriction of Saturn puts the pressure upon our energies so that we can see clearly what the problems are in our life. Saturn is sometimes referred to as the "planet of karma". Because of these energies, he is known as the "Great Teacher". Saturn's goal is to teach us in whatever way possible so we may spiritually evolve. It takes Saturn about 28 years to revolve around the sun. Where Saturn was in your birth chart is where he will be every 28 years. This is your Saturn return. Many people have many problems with health, jobs, and relationships during the 2 or so years of their Saturn return. When this happens, this is an opportunity to get your life in order where it needs to be. In this regard, think of it as a higher octave of a Mercury in retrograde. At the end of it, it is not about punishment, but forcing your to evolve or perish. Even if you want to or not.

Saturn rules

Constriction, Time, Sorrow, Death, Karma, Teaching, Lessons, Stability, Spiritual Growth, Decay, Removing Old Energies, Banishing

Color: Black

Number: 3

Herbs: Buckthorn, Cypress, Datura, Mullein, Myrrh, Scullcap, Solomon's Seal, Yew

Stones: Apache Tear, Black Tourmaline, Fossils, Hematite,

Obsidian, Smokey Quartz

Metal: Lead

Day: Saturday

Spirit: Aratron

Sephiroth: Binah

Ritual of the Septagram

The Ritual of the Septagram is a very powerful way to summon forth the magick of the planets. Its purpose is to infuse your temple space with the energy of the planet you wish to summon forth. The reason we want to place the planet's energy in your space is because it helps the spirits or angels of that planet manifest more easily. Think of it this way; if you were traveling in outer space and you wanted to visit an alien world then they must provide an atmosphere in which you could survive. You would need air that has plenty of oxygen so you could breath and the proper pressure so that you were not crushed by a denser atmosphere. You would also need a comfortable temperature so you would not freeze or burn to death. This is similar to what the spirits need. It is true, that the spirits do not HAVE to have their home planetary energy but it will make summoning them into your temple much easier without too much energy from you or them.

To begin with, we will summon the powers of the Kabbalistic Tree of Life into our body by superimposing the great tree over them. In many religious traditions it is said that the Creator, or the gods, made humans in their own image. If the Universe is the manifestation of the divine, then we have the Tree of life built in our energy bodies already. We humans are a microcosm of the Universe which is the tree of life. We will summon the energies by using the god name for each of the

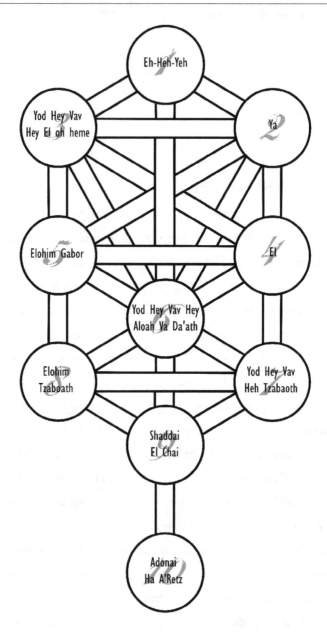

sephiroths. Yes, you can simply use the names of the sephiroth, but with this ritual you are placing the names of god, as it pertains to that sephiroth, in your body for power. To help you understand this, each god name listed in the Kabbalistic correspondences in chapter 3, is how God the Creator manifests in each of the sephiroth's. by empowering your own tree of life within yourself, you are becoming a microcosm of God. With this little power of god, you are able to control your universe and your destiny.

Part 1:

1. Connect with the Universe and the Creator of all things.

2. Imagine the white sphere of the sephiroth of Keter just above your head. Summon forth Divine light into Keter. If you like, you can point to each of the sephiroth spheres over your body. This will help your mind focus the energy in the appropriate place. Intone the Godname: **Eh-heh-yeh**

3. With your index finger or your magical dagger, draw a white line from Keter to the next sphere. Feel the energy flowing from Keter to Chokma. Imagine the gray sephiroth of Chokmah next to your Left Ear. Intone the Godname: **Ya**

4. Draw a white line of power from Chokma to the next sephiroth. As you continue to manifest the sephiroths over the body, continue to imagine the energies pouring into the next sephiroth. Imagine the black sephiroth of Binah next to your right ear. Intone the Godname: **Yod-hey-Vau-Hey El-oh-Heem**

5. Imagine the blue sephiroth of Chesed next to your left shoulder. Intone the Godname: **El**

6. Imagine the red sephiroth of Geburah next to your right shoulder.

Intone the Godname: **El-oh-heem Gah-bor**

7. Imagine the yellow sephiroth of Tiphereth at your heart center. Intone the godname: **Yod-hay-vau-hey El-oh-ah V-da-at**

8. Imagine the green sephiroth of Netzach next to your left hip. Intone the God Name: **Yod hay-vau-hey Tza-ba-oh-t**

9. Imagine the orange sephiroth of Hod next to your right hip. Intone the Godname: **El-oh-heem Tza-ba-oh-t**

10. Imagine the violet sephiroth of Yesod at your genitals. Intone the Godname: **Sha-di-el-chi**

11. Imagine the sephiroth of Malkuth at your feet. Half the sphere covers your feet and the other half is under the ground. Intone the Godname: **A-do-ny Ha-Ah'Retz**

12. Note: If you prefer, you may simply use the English names of the sephiroth, however, like I said, this ritual connects you to the divine in a very profound way and it makes planetary workings easier.

Dion Fortune in *The Mystical Qabalah* says, "The God-name represents the action of the Sephirah in the world of Atziluth, pure spirit; when the occultist invokes the forces of the Sephirah by the God-name, it means that he desires to contact its most abstract essence, that he is seeking the spiritual principle underlying and conditioning that particular mode of manifestation."

Part 2:

1. Go to the appropriate direction of the planet. Moon is West, Mercury is East, Venus is West, Sun is South, Mars is South, Jupiter is East, Saturn is North.

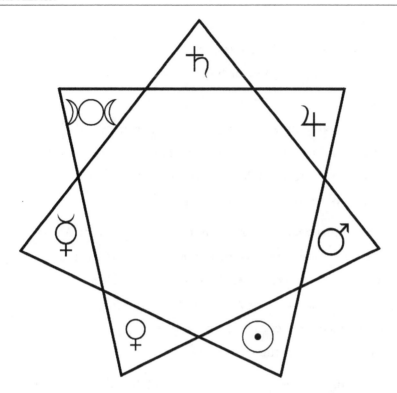

2. Draw the septagram in the air in the appropriate planetary color. You will begin and end with the point that marks the planet you want to evoke. Draw the planet clockwise. It may help to say the planet as you go around the septagram.

3. Perform the sign of the enterer by performing the following: Place your hands on either side of your ears, palms facing your head. Summon divine energy from the Universe to your crown chakra then see it go all the way down to your feet.

4. Point your hands toward the septagram at head level. This contains the divine energy in your body.

5. a. Inhale, to prepare to send the energy to the center of the

septagram.

b.   On the exhale, Take a step with your left foot and project
your hands to the center of the septagram (fingers pointing at the
center)

c.   at the same time, sending the energy from the Malkuth
sephiroth up to your heart and out of your hands. Make sure the
energy coming from Malkuth is the correct corresponding color
of the sephiroth.

d.   Send this energy to the center of the septagram. Visualize it
going out to the very edge of the universe. When you do this say
*ARARITA (god name of sephiroth that corresponds with planet. See
Chapter 3).* Example: For Mars you say *"Ararita Elohim Gabor "*, as
you see red energy coming from your feet up to your heart and out
of your hands into the septagram.

6. Then bring your right foot to meet your left and stomp! This
    proclaims the power you projected and your divine authority.

7. Draw a white line at the center of the septagram and trace a circle
    in the air clockwise   to the next direction. If you started in the
    East draw a white line in the air that connects the eastern
    septagram to the southern.

8. Perform steps 2-7 for the remaining three directions. You will
    have four septagrams, one in each direction, connected by a white
    line of energy. When finished say "This temple is open in the
    sphere of (appropriate sephiroth)

9. Using your own words, speak from your heart and call the plan-
    etary spirit you would like to work with.

10. Spend some time speaking with the planetary spirit, archangel, or

angel. Ask the spirit how you can work with it in a better or more profound way. My ritual is simply a guide. It is far better to work with the spirits in a way that is more pleasing to them."

Journey To Meet Planetary Spirit, Archangel, or Angel

When journeying to meet the planetary spirit, archangel, or angel, you will shamanically journey to the corresponding sephiroth just as you did when you were exploring the Kabbalistic Tree of Life as you did in Chapter 3. Remember that you can take the shortest route to the sephiroth, but you must journey through any sephiroth that lies on the path.

1. Decide which planetary spirit you would like to meet and commune with and the corresponding sephiroth. Spirits of the Moon are Yesod, spirits of Mercury are Hod, spirits of Venus are Netzach, spirits of the Sun are Tiphereth, spirits of Mars are Geburah, spirits of Jupiter are Chesed, spirits of Saturn are Binah. It is better to journey to that sephiroth on the corresponding planetary day, but not necessary to see results.

2. Light a candle in the correct sephiroth color and light incense that corresponds the the corresponding planet.

3. You may sit or lie down, then establish a shamanic trance space. Make the intention of meeting the spirit in question. You can say, " It is my intention to journey to (sephiroth) to meet (name of spirit).

4. Beginning with Malkuth, journey to the each of the sephiroth's on the path to the sephiroth of your destination.

5. Once there, spend a moment in the sephiroth and take in your surroundings.

6. Again, state your intention.

7. Visualize the spirit appearing before you.

8. Spend some time speaking with the planetary spirit, archangel, or angel. Ask the spirit how you can work with it in a better or more profound way. My ritual is simply a guide. It is far better to work with the spirits in a way that is more pleasing to them.

Planetary Conjuration/ Summoning

Planetary conjuration/ summoning in a shamanic style is a little different from modern ceremonial magick. You do not need all the ritual tools, circles, and barbarous conjurations. I prefer to use the corresponding candle color and incense of the planet, but I rarely use a lot of tools or regalia. The major tool you will need is your power of Will, Thought, Desire, Belief and Imagination. If you would like to use all the traditional ceremonial tools you certainly can. As long as you feel magical and powerful that is what is most important. If you have a strong power of imagination and astral sight then you can simply evoke the spirit in your ritual space. Sometimes it helps if you evoke them in a Triangle of Art. This helps condense the energy so the spirit can materialise better on the astral and etheric planes. If you are just learning this kind of magick and your powers of astral sight are not very strong yet, you can use a black magick mirror in your triangle of art. Most of the time, when we use a triangle of Art and magick mirror in the center, it is to bind the spirit in that location. This is not the case for our purposes. For us, we simply want to contain and condense the energies so that the spirit can manifest easier on the astral plane. You can also use a black bowl filled with water for scrying or a crystal ball. If you are using a magick mirror, then the mirror needs to be fastened to the triangle of art some way in the center and the Triangle should be facing up with the apex toward the ceiling. If you are using a crystal ball or scrying bowl the triangle of art can be laid flat with the apex away from you.

You will also want to invoke your patron god or goddess. Whichever one feels more appropriate to the work at hand. We will only be aspecting our god or goddess with this ritual. We do not want full on invocation, or possession, because we are not asking our god to the work for us, we are invoking a portion of their power so we may us it to better summon the spirit. If you feel you do not need to invoke your god to perform spirit invocation then you may try so without doing it. Try both ways and see which one is right for you.

When we summon planetary spirits, archangels, and angels we do not bind them to do tasks for us or bind them to appear in the triangle of art. We would only bind a demon and lesser chaotic spirits to our will, never angels and planetary spirits. These spirits we want a working relationship with and we do not want to force them to do something against their will. Most of these spirits are too powerful to bind anyway; you probably could not if you tried. Instead of binding them, we ask them and thank them for their help. We should treat all spirits with respect, even demons.

1. Decide on the spirit you would like to conjure/summon.

2. On the correct planetary day of the week, prepare your ritual space. If you need the Triangle and scrying tool (mirror, bowl, crystal ball) set up these tools now. If you are using a magick mirror, draw the spirit's sigil on the mirror using a black eye liner pencil. Remember, if you do not know what the spirit's sigil is, you can journey to them and ask for a symbol or sigil you may use to conjure them.

3. Perform the ritual of the Septagram parts 1 and 2.

4. Light the corresponding colored candle. You may use one or two candles and place them near the triangle of art. Light the planetary incense.

5. Aspect your god or goddess.

6. If you are using a scrying bowl or crystal ball, astrally trace the spirit's sigil over the ball or bowl. You can also astrally trace the septagram, beginning with the corresponding planet, over your scrying tool so they may manifest easier.

7. Summon the spirit with these words, or you may come up with words of your own. *"I summon (name of spirit) in the name of (god you invoked and any powers of wondrous deeds they have done). (Spirit name), come and appear before me and speak to me in a clear and tangible voice. I ask that you show yourself to me visibly (In this scrying tool if using) ."*

8. Allow the spirit a moment to manifest. You can aid in the manifestation by connecting to the energies of the planet and visualizing the spirit to appear before you. The spirit can use the visualization as a tool to help them manifest. If the spirit has not manifested, place more intense on the burner and repeat the summoning.

9. When the spirit has manifested say, *"(Name of spirit), I welcome you into my ritual space and thank you for coming. I would like to (state your intention)"*

10. You may now ask the spirit questions, ask for help with magick, or ask them to help you perform a task. Remember, the planetary spirits only do things that their planet is related to. You would not ask a spirit of Saturn to find you love.

11. When you are finished with the summoning say, *"(Spirit Name),*

thank you for helping me with (intention/ magick/ etc). I hope you will come
again and work with me in the art of magick. Thank you. Farewell."

12. See the spirit fading away. Extinguish the candles and incense.

13. Cleanse or banish your working space.

Planetary Candle Magick

Supplies Needed:

Colored Candle that corresponds to sephiroth that the planet governs.

Essential oil in the herb of planet

Number of Stones corresponding to planet (For example: 6 Tigers Eye
for The Sun)

Number of Herbs Corresponding to planet (Example: 6 different herbs
that relate to Sun)

1. On the corresponding day of the week, inscribe your candle with
   the symbol of the planet you are working with.

2. Take a moment to connect with the energies of the planet you are
   working with.

3. Anoint the candle with the planetary oil and visualize the outcome of your goal and place in the center of your working space.

4. Trace the septagram, beginning with the appropriate planet, over
   the candle.

5. With each stone, hold in your dominant hand and visualize your
   outcome. Send the energy into the stone. Place all stones around
   the candle.

6. Light the candle and visualize your outcome.

7. Using a mortar and pestle, grind each herb while visualizing your

outcome. At the same time sending energy through the pestle into the herb. The mortal acts as a magickal container to hold the energy.

8. Place the herbs around the candle and stones.

9. Spend some time visualizing your goal. If you like, you can burn the candle all at once or you may burn the candle a little on consecutive days that corresponds with the planet. For example: For the sun, starting on Sunday, burn the candle a little each day for 6 days. This will begin with the powers of the sun and each day add an additional planet. You can also burn the candle for 7 days if you like. For planets such as Saturn, you can burn the candle for 3 days or you can burn it on all 7 days to attract the energies of all 7 planets.

10. When the candle is burned down, take the remaining wax, herbs, and stones and place them in a sachet or mojo bag. Use the corresponding color. If you cannot find the correct color use white, black, or red.

9
Universal
and Spiritual Energies

The Cosmic Web

The Cosmic Web is an energetic link that connects all things in the Universe both physical and spiritual. We use the symbol of a spider's web to better understand this link. Everything in the Universe is connected. As with a spider's web, some things are very strongly connected because they are closer to each other, while other things are very far apart on the web and have a weaker connection, but are still connected. The Cosmic Web helps us understand how things like, The Law of Attraction, works. The law of attraction states that things that are similar are attracted to each other. Like attracts like. This is the law that allows sympathetic magick to work. For example, to attract money into your life you would surround yourself with coins, dollar bills, and pictures of money or things money can buy. It is also the reason we are able to call to the gods, perform long distance healing, and summon planetary energies. By tuning into the spirits and energies of a planet, you are able to establish a link via the Cosmic Web and summon forth and control the planetary energies. The Cosmic Web is what binds us spiritually together. We are linked on an astral, spiritual, and divine level. As we have discussed before, when we spiritually evolve on a personal level, we affect everyone as a whole; even if it's just a little bit at a time.

Karma

Karma is a very important energy to the spiritual minded person. Karma is a Sanskrit word that means *action*. Action means movement or to go forward. I suppose it could also mean to go backward. To "act" on something is to work for some sort of accomplishment or manifestation. When we apply this definition to our spiritual evolution, karma means to go forward in our spiritual path. How we do this depends on us. Karma does not mean "what comes around goes around". There are no beings in the heavens who have a magical score card and are keeping a tally about who does wrong and who does right. That is a Judeo-Christian concept. The universe does not punish per se. The universe seeks balance in order to for humanity, as well as all beings on the earth, and the entire multi-verse to evolve as a spiritual whole.

The word *karma* comes from Hinduism and Buddhism. In Hindu philosophy, the civil station where you were born is your destiny, or Dharma. If you were born to a poor family then it is your karma or destiny to be poor. If you were born into a rich family then it is your karma to be rich. In this culture, it is important to learn all the life lessons you can with the station that you are born in. Upon death, you will be reincarnated into the next civil station and learn those lessons. In the U.S., it is the American dream to work hard and change your station in life. We love hearing stories about the poor man who worked his way to the top and became rich. We may say it was his "karma" to become a rich man because he or she worked so hard. In Hinduism they do not believe that to always be the case. However, they do believe that you honor the gods by working hard and achieving success. They also believe it is good Karma to be a good person, be caring to others, serve your mother and father, and honor the spouse with the highest regard. When we look at karma like this, it is more about living an honorable life through working hard at your civil duties then necessarily spiritual development.

In the Western culture, karma has come to mean rewards and punishment. If I do good things then good things will happen to me, if I do bad things then bad things will happen to me. In my spiritual experience, I have not found this to be true. I have seen many caring, unselfish people get cancer and die as those who are cruel and selfish live a life of luxury. This is when we say the universe is unfair. In my experience, the universe cares nothing about being fair. The universe only cares about the spiritual development of all beings. In Wicca there is rede that says, "An it harm none, do what thou wilt. Otherwise what you do comes back to you three times." I know I will bust some balloons when I say I have never seen this to be true. I have blessed many people without a single blessings in return and I have cursed people to have absolutely nothing "bad" happen to me. Nothing. This is so for a few reasons. First, karma doesn't punish. Karma teaches. There is no buildup of energy with your name on it. There is no karma spirit that has a bag of energy that you put out and will dump on you as soon as they can.

Karma only wants to teach. Karma only wants to make you better as a spiritual being. The energies of the universe only strive to help you understand and learn. In essence, what happens is that the universe will send you the energies that you need in order to learn. So, for example, if you hit someone in the face and cause them harm, the universe will not send some random person to punch you in the face. If that were so, then we would be on an endless merry-go-round of people continually punching each other in the face. The better solution the universe has is to show you, in a very personal way, why you should be better than violence and rise above punching someone. Perhaps the universe gives you a scenario in your life where you begin to understand the pain violence causes someone. Maybe you meet someone who has been harmed and after hearing their story you try your hardest to not hurt anyone else. Maybe you witness someone else getting hurt and you are able to see the pain it causes. Or maybe you come to a point in your life where you simply understand violence does not solve problems. When you learn your spiritual lesson, that particular karma is resolved.

There are many different types of karma. One very powerful karma is our relationships to people and how they change us. There are those who come into our lives and teach us and there are those who have a profound effect on our lives. My theater teacher in high school, Judy Radigan, taught me how to be strong and speak my mind. She taught everyone in her classes to do the right thing and stand up for what you believe in. Growing up I had a bad stutter and I wanted to be an actor anyway. Ms. Radigan made me practice my lines and work very hard to obtain my goals. It was because of her that I was able to get many roles in high school and college productions. We have relationships with friends and lovers that affect us very deeply as well. It is unfortunate when we become bitter or resentful because of relationships. The universe works in very mysterious ways so perhaps it is our karma to be bitter and angry. Maybe it is part of our destiny to understand what pain and bitterness is. It does not mean we have to feel that way forever. Those of us who have felt those feelings and have grown from them understand what someone else is going through when they are feeling the resentfulness of relationships.

In my mind, ideally, relationships should open our minds and our hearts. They should teach us how to expand our spirits to be open to the wonders of the universe. When I was 23, I dated a man who was 35 years old. I felt a deep love for him that I never knew I was capable of having. I grew up in a family that loved each other but was not a family who often hugged or touched. That was normal for me. He, on the other hand, grew up in an Italian family who hugged and expressed their feelings all the time. When we would go out to parties and dance clubs he was surprised when I rarely touched or hugged any of our friends. He taught me that non-sexual loving touch was sacred and healing; especially for gay men. It was very awkward for me at first, but I grew used to it. After a time, I learned to open my heart to friends and hugging became the norm for me. Five years after that I became a successful massage therapist and healer.

What of the karma of cursing another? This is the question of a magical lifetime. In some magical communities, it is taught that we should never curse even if someone hurt us physically, mentally, emotionally, or spiritually. To do so would get the "karmic" effect of being cursed ourselves three times. I personally have found this to be untrue. When I was learning Traditional Witchcraft form my first teacher, I was taught that cursing another has no karmic repercussions if you feel 100% completely justified. For argument's sake, say someone harmed your child. If you cursed them so they would feel every amount of pain your child felt, then that curse would be justified. There would be no "backlash" or "backfire" from the spell. The energies of justice would prevail. I think that where magicians go wrong with such a curse is if they feel guilty about what they did. Whenever we think "oh, I shouldn't have done that" then we are placing negative energy in our aura and we are attracting the energies back that we sent out. Like attracts like, remember. I do not believe that anyone should curse another just because we are angry at someone. But, if you feel that you are truly justified, then the karma is on them, not you.

One of the most powerful energies in the world is forgiveness. Forgiveness does not mean that you allow someone to hurt you. Or you saying it was okay for another person to harm you. Forgiveness means that you are no longer holding on to the negative energy that binds the karma of another to you through bitterness and anger. Remember the roll of karma is spiritual evolution. Nothing more. Nothing less. Every spirit and every being must eventually evolve. It may take millions, if not billions, of years but that is the destiny of all things. When we hang on to anger, we are energetically binding another person to us. In

Luciferian mythology, because Lucifer holds onto his anger with God for banishing him from heaven, he is forever bound with the karma and fate of God. When we forgive someone we are releasing the energetic cords that bind us to another. Also, by holding on to anger we are binding someone to their current state of awareness and not allowing someone to evolve into a higher being. I understand that when someone hurts you so deeply that you have trouble letting the pain and anger go. At the end of the day, by forgiving others we are allowing them space to become better people so they will not hurt someone else like they hurt us.

Divine Will

Everything in the Universe has a spark of the divine. From humans to angels and to every animal on earth. The oceans, mountains, deserts and every plant and stone also have an aspect of the All. We are connected through Spirit and our relationship to the earth and the cosmos. We often hear the saying, "It's the Will of God". It is said that the Source of All Creation has a divine master plan. Our Creator is the ultimate creative source. We are divine in our own right and so, too, have the divine creative spark with us. But it is more than creating something or *working*. It is our great reason for being.

Our Divine Will is the great spiritual purpose for incarnating on earth. It is the reason why we are alive today. In Ceremonial Magical circles, it is sometimes called "The Great Work". For magical people, we know in our beings that we are meant to do more than average people. We are spiritually evolving beings that seek to connect to the energies of the Universe and to help others. Some people believe that you make a soul contract in the spirit world to do something that helps others on the physical plane. Yes, part of this soul contract is to learn certain lessons so that you become more spiritually aware and evolved. The

Divine Will is that greater purpose that propels you on your spiritual path. Some of us learn our Divine Will early in life while others may take many years to find it. Remember, time has no meaning in the world of spirit and the Universe is in no hurry for spiritual evolution. It takes as long as it takes.

Reincarnation

Many cultures around the world believe in reincarnation, specifically, Buddhist, Hindus, Pagans, and many magical practitioners. As most of us know, reincarnation is the theory that we are reborn to this world many times, stretching out many time periods. There are many different beliefs how this may occur. Some people believe that the very first life you have is that of a rock, then plant, bug, animal, human, then perhaps to that of an ascended being or an angel. Others believe that your first life is human and your last life is a human.

Let us for a moment discuss the purpose for reincarnation. If we remember back to the beginning of this book you will remember that one of the purposes of creation, itself, is so that The Creator can fully understand itself with the many dynamics of relationships. Relationships bring about challenges, struggles, triumph, love, and happiness. Every person in every culture and every times period has their own individual experience on how these things occur, which include the individual thought process and actions taken or not taken. In order to have all of these myriad of experiences reincarnation must take place. Another reason is that, like we have said before, that evolution of life must take place.

Every species must eventually evolve in order to get back to the wholeness of creation. Every life, from animal to human and perhaps vegetable and mineral, must transform itself to become greater than it is. Once this happens, we will return to the All, that which created all things, with many experiences and wisdom so that we (as part of the All) can be part of a greater evolved being. This may take many lifetimes over hundreds and thousands of years to complete. One cannot know all there is to know and experience in just one life in one country. As I have done the research for this book and for *Underworld,* I have found that there are many experiences from cultures that I will never have in my current life as I know it now. Even simply traveling in the United States alone, there are major differences between American culture from the South to the Southwest, to the East Coast to the West Coast. That would be several lifetimes in just one country.

If you look around your daily life, you will see many people who are selfish, greedy, and do not understand the suffering of others. This is evident of a young soul. For some, it takes many life times for this understanding. We should have understanding and compassion for new souls as well as try to teach them the best we can. I have found to teach by modeling behaviors is the best way to do so. When they are ready they will learn. Not until then. When we see some of our politicians and leaders make decisions based on the greed of power, and not the benefit of all, we can see the evidence that they are new souls. Unfortunately, they are more troublesome than the average new soul because they are in a position of power and each unenlightened decision affects their people and perhaps the world.

I believe that if you are a shaman, witch, or magician, then you have had many lives before. Perhaps you were one or more of these things in a past life. I have found that if you gravitated to magick at an early age, or were at least interested in magick and healing, then you have lived a magical life before. Yes, in ancient pagan cultures such as the Egyptians, Native Americans, Nordics, and so on magick was a part of everyday life, but the Priest, Shaman, or Cunning Person was indeed special to each of their communities. There are also many lives to be had as a magical person as well. As a teacher and ritual leader, I have worked with many people at many different levels of magical ability. Those of greater magical skills are no more important than those of less magical skill, it simply means they may have had more lives to experience and practice their talent.

What of finding out who you were in a past life? Both Hindus and Buddhist believe that this is unnecessary and a waste of time. The thought behind this is that you have already learned what you needed to know from these lives and to go over it again would be like a high school student re-doing the 3rd grade. You may not directly remember the lessons you have learned, but it has been imprinted on your spirit. For example, because of your experience from a past life you no longer need to be taught to treat people with compassion. You instinctively do so in this life. There is no need to relive that life again. Also, there is a tendency of some people to become fixated with one or more of their past lives. It can be a way to place blame on something for a shortcoming in this life. Yes, you may learn that in a past life you were rich and had servants and that may be one of the reasons who hate working in this life. What is the point of learning that in a past life? The point is to work through that and find joy in making your own way in this life.

Some people may want to find out how famous they were in a past life. Were you royalty? Where you a priestess on the isle of Avalon? Where you a famous Roman Warrior? Maybe. Maybe not. We all cannot have lives such as this. But it is possible. There is little benefit of finding out about a fantastic life you once lived. Our time is better spent cultivating our magical and healing skills now to help the people who need it in this life.

But what of karma from a past life that is manifesting in this life. Our current lives are meant to be lived in the present. Otherwise, we would remember vividly all of our past lives. The karmas and lessons that are needed to be learned in an authentic and organic way. Learning of "why" our karma from a past life has manifested in this life may only complicate matters. We must focus on where we are now and what is the task at hand.

The Buddhist believe that in order to become free of the Wheel of Life, Death, and Rebirth is to find *Liberation*. To be liberated means that you have no karmic attachment, or lessons needed to be learned, and you may join the Universal whole. In the *Tibetan Book of the Dead*, there is a list of things to know and do to prevent yourself from returning to the world of the living. It is quite literally an instruction book for the dead to avoid reincarnation. You must avoid certain lights which represent attachments to worldly things and desires. You must also travel the spiritual planes with a sense of peace, love, and compassion. Otherwise, your fear and anger will lead you back to the Wheel of Reincarnation.

Once you are liberated, you have a few choices on how you want to remain in the spiritual world. You may connect with the All and lose yourself in the bliss of your creator. The Second option is that you can join the All, yet retain your consciousness of the self. The last option is to become a spiritual guide or teacher to those on earth who need your guidance. I personally believe that is a wonderful option. I am very grateful to my teachers and guides in spirit.

Dark Night of the Soul

One of the most spiritually challenging things you will experience is the Dark Night of the Soul. The reason it is called the Dark Night of the

Soul is because in times past, before you were to be married, knighted, or join a religious organization you had to spend an entire night alone contemplating your endeavor. This was done to make certain that the path that lay before you was the correct path for you. Many spiritual traditions require the seeker to meditate upon their chosen path before they go forward. This is especially done before initiations and trials that will elevate the seeker to a new spiritual level. In modern times, this is more of a spiritual challenging time to one's life rather than just one night.

There comes a point upon your spiritual path that you may become dissatisfied, frustrated, and angry. You have achieved so much upon your path then you may realize that your life is not what you thought it would be. You may have lost your job, ended a relationship, experienced health problems, or had to move away. It manifests differently for everyone. Sometimes, when we begin our path we may have dreams of a better life. We may fantasize about magical power, status, money, or any other thing that magick, and a life devoted to spirit, could bring us. As you may know by now, this is not how spirituality works. I do not believe that life is about suffering, but our lives are made up of challenges that we must continually face. But sometimes, those challenges can become overwhelming and become too much to bare. We may say to ourselves, "I am devoted to the gods, then why is my life not what I wanted it to be."

This can be a hard pill to swallow. I have seen many magical/ spiritual students find themselves in this state. I can remember when I was a student and I would work so hard in my magical and spiritual studies. I did everything I was supposed to do. My relationships ended and I lost my job which I liked very much. I spent the winter of 2003 hitting the Chicago streets filling out job applications and going online looking for anything I could do for work. I was miserable. The gods and spirits had seemed to abandon me. I was angry and frustrated. I had cast job spells and did my god devotions and nothing materialized. I took a management position at a video store. It was one of the worst jobs I had ever had. The pay was awful and the hours were late. It was kind of funny because I worked so many hours I had very little time to watch movies and customers would get very angry when I could not give them a review of the latest movie release. Apparently, this is very important when you are running a video store.

In May of 2003 I took a sales job at Guess when it was on Michigan Avenue in Chicago. I was good at men's fashions and it paid a lot more than the video store. Go figure a gay man would be good at fashion. Finally, on Samhain of 2003, my former teacher and now colleague, Matthew Ellenwood, and my friend Kamion, and I were speaking with the the spirits on the Talking Board when the question was raised, "Should Chris learn Reiki to begin his healer path?"

"No." The board spelled out. "Massage Therapy". January of 2004 I began massage therapy school and I had never been happier. Finally, after more than a year I had found my path. I still had challenges that year, but my path was becoming more clear. I had learned the magick, the techniques, and the discipline, but I was lost because I had no outlet to practice it. Later that same year, seven of us founded The Brotherhood of the Phoenix that eventually evolved into the Fellowship of the Phoenix.

The Dark Night of the Soul has been so hard for some magical practitioners that I have seen some throw away their tools and live a "normal" life. Shamanism and witchcraft is very challenging. It will not "fix" our problems, but it does give us the tools to help us through and hopefully grant us wisdom to make the correct choices for us. The Dark

Night also is not a one time occurrence. It can happen many times in our magical lives. I know that may not be what you want to hear but it is true.

I want to take a moment to talk about the IAO formula. "I" is for Isis, the Great Mother who nurtures us. When we begin our magical paths, we are excited and full of vigor. We are learning everything we can about magick and the gods. It may seem like we have a charmed life. Everything falls into place. The gods and spirits are opening the path to us and helping us on our journey. The mother energies are nurturing us. Think about how when we plant the seed we are lovingly planting it in the earth making sure it has plenty of water and sunlight.

The "A" is for Apophis, the Destroyer. After the mother energies have given us our tools she abandons us. We have all the tools and resources we need and the nurturing energies withdraw. We are left alone. Our charmed life is over. The thing is no one has told us about our new fate and it can be heartbreaking to discover that our once loving gods and spirits are silent. When this happened to me, I felt very abandoned and betrayed. What did I do wrong? I thought. What I did not understand at the time was that the gods were kicking me out of the nest so that I may learn to fly on my own. You learn magick to not be controlled by the energies but for YOU to control the energies of the Universe. During this time, there were many mistakes I made. I would try doing things how I have always done them and they were not working. I had to use trial and error to come up with new ways of doing things. Think about the seed that is in the earth. Our planter is gone and it is up to us to become uncomfortable in our seed and painfully burst from our dark prison and struggle through the soil to reach sunlight at the top.

The "O" is for Osiris, the resurrected God. The energies that destroyed our old ways of doing things have taught us how to be our own person and use our magical tools how we see fit. We still make mistakes and our journey is not over, but we are no longer dependent on our teachers or the spirits and we continue upon our magical path.

When I became a massage therapist it opened up many doors for me. I became a Reiki Master and master energy healer. I had found my path and my spiritual calling. Returning to the planted seed analogy, the plant finally reaches the top of the soil and is fed by the light of the sun. Through this the flowers grow and the true potential of the seed is realized.

I think part of the energies of the Dark Night of the Soul is to ask us, "Is this what we really want? It won't be easy. Are you willing to go further?" For myself, I cannot ignore the call of the spirits. In some shamanic societies, it is believed that to ignore the call of the spirits is to invite sickness and death. The universe put you on the physical plane for a reason. If you reject that reason the universe may call you back home and put someone else in your place. I do not necessarily believe that philosophy. I think that you are free to live your life how you see fit. Even if you choose to work with the spirits or not.

If you find yourself with the energies of the Dark Night, my advice to you is to do the best you can. If you need to take a short magical break then do so. If you need to continue your magical studies then do so. Ask your guides and gods for assistance, but be prepared that you may have to do this all by yourself. Be kind to yourself and allow yourself to make mistakes and to learn from them. If you hurt someone, try your best to fix it. If someone hurts you, learn from it. Have compassion for your experience and for yourself. The Dark Night of the Soul will challenge you to your spiritual core, but it will give you a lot of spiritual insight as well. One of the things that we can learn from mythology is that many heroes and gods face the Dark Night themselves during their journey. Hercules had his twelve labors, King Author had to find the Holy Grail, Isis searched Egypt for the body parts of Osiris, and Odin wandered Midgard. It is through these challenges that magick, wisdom, and healing occur. Joseph Campbell says in his book, *The Power of Myth,* "One thing that comes out in myths, for example, that at the bottom of the abyss comes the voice of salvation. The black moment is the moment when the real message of transformation is going to come. At the darkest moment comes the light."

Fate and Destiny

One of the reasons we journey to the Upperworld is find out about our Fate and Destiny. Some people feel that fate and destiny are the same thing, but from my experience it is not. Fate is the outcome of your past and present actions. One could say it can be related to karma. If you are sick and you take medicine you are fated to get well. Likewise, if you are sick and you allow disease to take over your body then you are fated to die. From a magical point of you, your fate is the result of your spiritual work, meditations, and your magick. Destiny, on the other hand is what you are meant to be. Your destiny can be to become a healer, teacher, leader, or shaman. In New Age teachings, while you are in between lives, you make a spiritual contract with the universe to reincarnate for a specific divine purpose according to your will. For instance, you may have a spiritual contract to come to earth to become a healer or magical teacher so that you may help people spiritually evolve.

If you are reading this book and interested in being a shaman or walking a shamanic path, then it is possible that it is your destiny to be a shaman in this life. Some believe that we choose this destiny ourselves, while others believe that you are chosen by the gods or spirits to be a shaman. I believe that those of us who pursue a path of spiritual evolution and healing we cannot help but to want to walk a shamanic path when we incarnate upon the earth. I do not think we take it lightly in the spirit world when we are in between lives. I also think it is apart of our natural progression as spiritual beings.

There are many shamans who say that they are chosen by the spirits to become a shaman and it was not their "choice". Perhaps. I do not think the spirits randomly pick someone to become a shaman nor do they pick someone who would be their favorite. I think the spirits recognize our spirits in this incarnation and recognize someone who is a healer or a shaman life after life. We chose this path. We just may not remember doing so in the spirit world.

There is something that is called the "shaman's sickness". This is when a person becomes deathly ill or has a mental crisis. They are usually ill for a few days and sometimes incoherent or having fever dreams. During this time, the spirits come for the shaman to be and rebuilds their body and gives them magical power to work with the spirits. If one does not heed, or fights against, their destiny then the sickness never resolves only gets worse. The shamanic candidate continues to become more and more ill and can even die. Mental health professionals, who walk a shamanic path, believe that this may be one of the reasons that some people have mental health problems. Because they are ignoring their destiny; their mind deteriorates. I think that this can certainly be the case but not always. The gods have given us free will and therefore have the free will to say no. We have the option to live healthy lives that do not involve magick and the spirits. But what a pity if we did this.

There are many people who call themselves "shaman" and do not walk with the spirits. I wonder at times if some people are confused about what shaman actually means. I have found that some men who are pagan, or spiritually inclined, like that word. They do not want to be called a witch and pagan does not sound correct either for them. They may read books about shamanism but rarely practice and refine their techniques.They may take a few classes with a teacher never to finish. This is okay. What this simply means is that it is not their destiny to be a shaman. Perhaps their destiny is to be a healer or some other form of spiritual person. Sometimes our Fate and Destiny hits us in the face. Other times it is up to us to meditate, take classes, read books, and experiment with different traditions to find the spiritual destiny that is right for us.

I found magick and shamanism at a very young age. I was seventeen. I studied everything I could get my hands on. I read books on witchcraft and magick, played spirit boards, and got formal magical training at the age of 25. I went further and further in my magical studies and development. Nothing was more important. At 28 at went back to school to become a professional massage therapist. From there, I became a Reiki Master and professional energy healer. At this same time I was on the board of directors for The Brotherhood of the Phoenix, a pagan spiritual group for men who love men, and an ordained minister.

With everything I was doing, I was becoming overwhelmed and realized I had no personal life and I was barely 30 years old. No romantic life to speak of and I barely saw friends. My life consisted of working six days a week and any time off was focused on The Brotherhood or helping others. I wanted to stop. I wanted to reclaim myself for myself and just be me. I got off the board and just took a rest. I still worked massaging and healing others but I did magick at a bare minimum. I started dating and felt like I was seven years behind. The gods felt silent. After a couple of months people would randomly come to me needed my help. Sometimes they needed my healing abilities, other times they needed my magick abilities. There were friends who needed me to banish ghosts or heal their loved ones. There were also the call from spirit, the otherworld that needed my help or wanted to further my magical development. Each time I did healing work or magick I felt alive and connected. I felt like the universe was working through me. I was never so joyful as I was doing my best magical work. When I was overwhelmed I thought that magick was taking too much of a toll on me and being selfish with what it wanted. I figured out that it wasn't magick that was too much; it was that I had agreed to have too many responsibilities at once. Once I found a balance with everything I was doing in my life then I was happy. I was no longer fighting against my own destiny. I was using the magick of the scales and finding balance.

EXERCISE: Finding Your Destiny

1. Journey to the Upperworld and ask to speak with your Upperworld Guide or God.

2. Ask them to show you your destiny in this life.

3. They may show you an astral contract or a video of what you are supposed to do or simply tell you.

4. Be open to possibilities that you have never thought of.

5. Ask your guide or god to set you on the path of achieving your destiny. Remember, you have Free Will. If you do not choose to follow your spiritual chosen path you do not have to. However, I have found when you do it is a life that is very fulfilling.

6. When ready, come back to your body.

7. Give offerings and thanks to your guide and/or god.

The More Powerful You Become

The more powerful you become the more powerful spirits and entities will take notice of you. This can be both good and bad. When you first learn magick and shamanism you learn the very basics of magick. You learn the four elements, the basics of astrology, tarot, and intro to magick. There are many people who do this and never go any further. I think this is Okay. If someone is happy where they are and spiritually fulfilled then that is wonderful. For others, our quest into magick, shamanism, and spirituality is never ending and only becomes deeper the more we study, learn, and practice.

There comes a point in our magical and spiritual training that we become advanced magicians. We are now able to summon the dead, invoke the gods, and manipulate the world according to our Divine Will. This is when powerful entities and gods take notice of you. Some spirits may have been watching you your whole life. Some simply observe while others take an active role in aiding your progress. There many spirits, such as the Fates and Norns, that are actively weaving the web of life, death, and creation. They do not like having a magician, especially one who cannot see the whole picture, undoing what they have already done. Remember back to the myth of Asculapius and what Zeus did to him? This does not mean that every time you do great works of magick that the Universe is going to conspire against you. What this means is that you will be noticed.

Many years ago, I learned to do a very powerful form of dragon magick. It was very powerful and it took three advanced witches to do it. It was a powerful and amazing experience. I was told that it could only be done by at least three witches. It was impossible to do it alone. A year later, I was by myself while the others were away. I wanted to do magick that was powerful and life changing. But I was alone. I stood on the sacred hill and I felt the magick build up within me. I remembered the working. Yes! I remembered! I wanted to do the dragon magick. But it would not work. I was alone. But what if I could do it? What if I had the power? Being magical meant experimenting, I thought. Alone, I did the dragon magick. Holy shit! I did it.

But then, appearing before me in spirit, were three robed and hooded figures. They did not speak directly, but I could hear their voices in my head. "You have performed magick so few could do before. You must come and join us."

"Who are you? Where are you from?"

"We are part of the council of the Underworld," they said. "Your magick can be weaved with our own."

Needless to say I had no intention of permanently joining anyone in the Underworld. My answer was no. From time to time the triad would appear and observe me, watching my magical progress. After a few years of this I had to demand that they leave me be, which they did. I intuited that their intentions were not to harm me but to follow the magick.

Another time, I had journeyed far out into the depths of the universe. When I returned to my body, there was a strange spirit who had followed me home. It was silent with eyes dark and strange. It had no mouth so it did not speak. I tried to magically banish it. It would not be banished. I used a more powerful banishing technique. Still nothing. It quietly observed me for sometime. Then as quietly as it appeared, it faded away. I never saw it again.

Many of the spirits who take notice of you do not wish you harm, but some do. There are many beings out there that see you as a threat. Often times, they are other magicians or dark witches who have succumbed to their ego and see you as a rival or a threat. I never really understood why. I have always been happy on my own spiritual journey and never was threatened by anyone else. If a teacher was not a right fit then I went elsewhere. It is true when they say the teacher appears when the student is ready. But, because of my progress, I have been attacked in my dreams and cursed by other magicians. Luckily for me, I am loyal to my friends and my gods so if I ever needed help I always received it. However, if at all possible, I prefer to handle things like that myself.

There is really no way around this. My best advice to you is to be kind and respectful to all beings be they spiritual, animal, or human. Make sure to love your gods and do devotions and honor the ancestors every day. You still may have spirits and magicians challenge you, but you will have an arsenal at your disposal. Kindness is a far better weapon than magick.

Conclusion

Working with the spirits and energies of the Upperworld are very fulfilling and can speed up your spiritual progress a great deal. These energies are meant to help and guide you, but you have to do the work on your own; the gods cannot do it for you. But once you have obtained gnosis and wisdom, what then? I personally believe that we are put here on this earth to help people so they, too, can spiritually evolve and grow. How we help our community is up to you. Some people choose to be healers, shamans, energy workers, etc. while others wish to teach. I think whatever your destiny is in this life you should try to embrace it to the best of your ability. You are not perfect and do not try to be. Try to be the best you can. What that means is that your magical journey may not seem to be perfect. You may not feel like your magical journey is giving you a "charmed" life. You will experience ups and downs both magically and personally that may have you questioning your path. But what if that IS a perfect path for you. As you are probably aware, spiritual growth comes from our mistakes and our failures. It is true, that you do not always have to fail to succeed, but when you do fail, learn the lesson. Take a moment to grieve for your failure then go back and figure out the lesson.

Learning a magical lesson can be painful. It can bring you to your lowest and you may or may not overcome...at that moment. Eventually, we do overcome. Eventually, something within us kicks in and we have that "Ah-ha!" moment. I cannot count the times I have said to myself, "Oh, I just got that!" or "Why didn't I figure that out sooner?" Lessons are not a race. We figure things out at our own pace when we are ready. Sometimes we summon the gods and feel empowered and sometimes we summon the gods to help us get out of the mess we got ourselves in. The important things is that we keep going until we figure it out.

While we are walking along our path we should help others along the way. We should teach, heal, write, speak, and have magical conversations with those who need our help. The Universe wants us to have information, but it only gives us magical knowledge when we are ready. Sometimes it feels like we will never be truly ready. Well, here we are at the end of the Upperworld book. I think you are ready.

Next:
Shamanism, Myth, and Magick: Midworld

The next book in this series will be the Midworld. We will learn about the world around us, which includes nature spirits, elves, faeries, and the many spirits that make up the earth which we call home. There are many powers of the land that can strengthen our magical power as well as help us heal.

Bibliography

27 Stars, 27 Gods: The Astrological Mythology of Ancient India. Vic DiCara (Vraja Kishor). CreateSpace Indipendent Publishing Platform. 2012.

Angels, Demons, and Gods of the New Milennium. Lon Milo DuQuette. Samuel Weisner, Inc.1997.

Aradia or the Gospel of the Witches. Charles G. Leland. A new translation by Mario Pazzaglini, Ph.D. and Dina Pazzaglini. Phoenix Publishing. 1998

Ascension: Connecting With the Immortal Masters and the Beings of Light. Susan Shumsky, DD. New Page Books. 2010.

Asklepis: The Cult of The Greek God of Medicine. Alice Walton, Ph.D. Kessinger Publishing. 1893

Astrology: A Cosmic Science. Isabel M. Hickey. CRCS Publications. 1992.

The Books of Enoch: The Angels, The Watchers, and The Niphilim (with extensive commentary on The Three Books of Enoch, The Fallen Angels,The Calendar of Enoch, and Daniel's Prophecy). Joseph B. Pumpkin. Fifth Estate Publishers. 2011.

The Book of Fallen Angels. Michael Howard. Capallbann Publishing. 2004.

The Book of Solomon's Magick. Carroll "Poke" Runyon, M.A. The Church of the Hermetic Sciences, Inc. 1996.

A Breif History of Time: From the Big Bang to Black holes. Stephan W. Hawking. Bantam Books. 1988.

The Chicken Qabalah of Rabbi Lammed Ben Clifford. Lon Milo DuQuette. Weisner Books. 2001.

Courageous Dreaming: How Shamans Dream the World Into Being. Alberto Villoldo. Ph.D. Hay House, Inc. 2008.

Cunningham's Encyclopedia of Crystal, Gem, and Metal Magic. Scott Cunningham. Llewellyn Publications. 2001.

Cunningham's Encyclopedia of Magical Herbs. Scott Cunningham. Llewellyn Publications. 2000.

A Dictionary of Angels, Including the Fallen Angels. Gustav Davidson. Free Press. 1967.

Drawing Down the Spirits: The Traditions and Techniques of Spirit Possession. Kenaz Filan and Raven Kaldera. Destiny Books. 2009.

Egyptian Mythology: A Guide to the Gods, Goddesses, and Traditions of Ancient Egypt. Geraldine Pinch. Oxford University Press. 2002.

Finding Soul on the Path of Orisha: A West African Spiritual Tradition. Tobe Melora Correal. Crossing Press. 2003.

Five Lectures on Reincarnation. Swami Abhedananda. A Public Domain Book

From Distant Days: Myths, Tales, and Poetry of Ancient Mesopotamia. Translated with Introduction and Notes by Benjamin R. Foster. 1995.

Fundamentals of the Yoruba Religion Orisa Worship (Revised Edition). Chief FAMA. Ille Orunmila Communications. 1993.

A Garden of Pomegranates: Skrying on the Tree of Life. Isreal Regardie. Edited and Annotated with New Material by Chic Cicero and Sandra Tabatha Cicero. Llewellyn Worldwide. 1995.

The Haitian Vodou Handbook: Protocols for Riding with the Lwa. Kenaz Filan. Destiny Books. 2007

Handbook of Chinese Mythology. Lihui Yang and Deming An with Jessica Anderson Turner. Oxford University Press. 2005.

History and Mythology of the Aztecs: The Codex Chimalpopoca. Translated from the Nahuatl by John Beirhorst. The University of Arizona Press. 1992.

How To Read The Akashic Records: Accessing the Archive of the Soul and Its Journey. Linda Howe with Juliette Looye. Sounds True Inc. 2009.

Indian Mythology: Tales, Symbols, and Rituals from the Heart of the Subcontinent. Devdutt Pattanaik. Inner Traditions. 2003.

Karma and Reincarnation. Paramhansa Yogandanda. Crystal Clarity Publishers. 2007.

Karma-Yoga and Bhakti-Yoga. Swami Vivekananda. Ramakrishna-Vivekananda Center of New York.

Kali: The Black Goddess of Dakshinewar. Elizabeth U. Harding. 1993.

The Key of Solomon The King (Clavicula Salomonis). Translated and edited from manuscripts in the British Museum by S. Liddell MacGregor Mathers. Samuel Weisner, Inc. 1972.

Lakota Belief and Ritual. James R. Walker. Edited by Raymond J. DeMallie and Elaine A. Jahner. University of Nebraska Press. 1980, 1991.

Land of the Fallen Star Gods: The Celestial Origins of Ancient Egypt. J.S. Gordon. Bear and Company. 1997.

The Lost Art of Enochian Magic: Angels, Invocations, and the Secrets Revealed to Dr. John Dee. John DeSalvo, Ph.D. Destiny Books. 2010.

The Luminous Stone: Lucifer in Western Esotericism. Edited by Michael Howard and Daniel A. Schulke. Three Hands Press. 2016.

Madame Blavatsky: The Mother of Modern Spirituality. Gary Lachman. Jeremy P. Tarcher/ Penguin. The Penguin Group. 2012.

Magic of the Ordinary: Recovering the Shamanic In Judaism. Gershon Winkler. North Atlantic Books. 2003.

The Masks of God: Primitive Mythology. Joseph Cambell. Penguin Compuss. 1959.

Modern Magick: Twelve Lessons in the High Magickal Arts, Revised and Expanded. Donald Michael Kraig. 2010.

The Mystical Qabalah. Dion Fortune. Weiser Books. 1935.

The Mythology and Religion of the Aztec. Dr. Jesse Harasta and Charles River Editors. CreateSpace Indipendant Publishing. 2014.

Myths of Greece and Rome. Thomas Bulfinch. Penguin Books. 1979.

Norse Mythology. Neil Gaiman. W.W. Nortan and Company. 2017.

Orpheus and Greek Religion. W.K.C. Guthrie. Princeton University Press. 1952.

Our Troth (Second Edition): Volume 2 Living The Troth. Members of the Troth and Other True Folk Compiled by Kveldulf Gundarsson. BookSurge Publishing. 2007.

Parallel Worlds: A Journey Through Creation, Higher Dimensions, and the Future of the Cosmos. Michio Kaku. Anchor Books. 2004.

The Pathworker's Guide To the Nine Worlds. Raven Kaldera. Asphodel Press. 2006.

Pathways To Bliss: Mythology and Personal Transformation. Joseph Campbell. New World Library. 2004

Peter and Wendy. J.M. Barrie. Charles Scribner's Sons. 1911.

Philip's Atlas of the Universe. Patrick Moore. Astronomer Royal. 1991-1994.

The Picatrix: Liber Atratus Edition. Translated by John Michael Greer and Christopher Warnock. Adocentyn Press. 2010-11.

Planetary Magick. Melita Denning and Osborne Phillips. Llewellyn Publications. 1992.

The Power of Myth. Joseph Campbell with Bill Moyers. Anchor Books. 1988.

The Practice of Dream Healing: Bringing Ancient Greek Mysteries into Modern Medicine. Edward Tick, Ph.D. Quest Books. 2001.

Prayer, Magic, and the Stars In the Ancient and Late Antique World. Edited by Scott Noegel, Joel Walker, and Brannon Wheeler. The Pennsylvania State University Press. 2003.

Shamanism: Archaic Techniques of Ecstasy. Mircea Eliade. Penguin Books. 1964.

Shamanism and Spirituality in Therapeutic Practice: An Introduction. Christa Mackinnon. Singing Dragon. 2012.

Spirit Conjuring For Witches: Magical Evocation Simplified. Frater Barrabbas. Llewellyn Publications. 2017.

Star Lore: Myths, Legends, and Facts. William Tyler Olcott. Dover Publications. 2004.

Stars of the First People: Native American Star Myths and Constellations. Dorcus S. Miller. Pruett Publising. 1997.

Stellar Magic. Payam Nabarz. Avalonia. 2009.

Stonehenge: A New Interpretation of Prehistoric Man and the Cosmos. John North. The Free Press. 1996.

The Temple of the Cosmos: The Ancient Egyptian Experience of the Sacred. Jeremy Naydler. Inner Traditions International. 1996.

Theogony and Works of Days. Hesiod. Stephany Nelson and Richard Cardwell. Focus Publishing. 2009.

The Tibetan Book of the Dead. Robert A.F. Thurman. Bantam Books. 1994.

Underworld: Shamanism, Myth, and Magick. Chris Allaun. Mandrake of Oxford. 2017.

A Walk Through The Heavens: A Guide to Stars and Constellations and Their Legends. Third Edition. Milton D. Heifetz and Wil Tirion. Cambridge Universtiy Press. 2004.

Yezidis: The History of a Community, Culture, and Religion. Birgul Acikyildiz. I.B. Taurus and Co. 2015.

Yoga and Vedic Astrology: Sister Sciences of Spiritual Healing Essentials of Vedic Astrology-Volume I. Sam Geppi (Sadasiva). Vedic Academy Press. 2015.

Websites

http://www.golden-dawn.org/secret_chiefs_second_order.html

Index

A

Aaru 65
Abyss 50, 239
Adam 132, 134
Aesculapius 163, 164, 176
Afterlife 21
Agni 172
Aiwass 149
Akasha 61, 73
Akashic Records 61
Alchemy 74, 119, 146, 195
Aldebaran 169, 172
Aluminum 208
Amun 46
Ancestors 13, 14, 15, 20, 31, 51,
    56, 64, 91, 116, 129, 149,
    150, 173, 245
Andromeda 61, 175, 176
Angelic 8, 48, 68, 115, 119, 123,
    127, 128, 130, 135, 136, 137,
    138, 140
  Magick 116, 119, 129
Angels 8, 11, 14, 15, 20, 21, 26,
    31, 46, 57, 60, 68, 70, 72,
    73, 74, 75, 76, 77, 79, 80,
    81, 82, 113, 114, 115, 116,
    118, 120, 121, 123, 124, 125,
    126, 127, 128, 129, 130, 132,
    134, 136, 139, 140, 141, 158,
    159, 160, 212, 219, 230
Animal 31, 32, 33, 34, 35, 89,
    101, 106, 191, 230, 231, 245
Anshar 38
Anu 38, 64
Apache 162, 166, 193, 194, 211
Aphrodite 76
Apollo 23, 77, 95, 105, 163, 164
Apophis 237
Aquarius 185
Araquiel 122

Aratron 212
Archangel 48, 68, 70, 72, 73, 74,
    75, 76, 77, 79, 80, 81, 82,
    115, 116, 118, 119, 120, 121,
    123, 126, 131, 140, 158, 160,
    170, 217, 219
Archetypes 21
Ares 78, 189
Arianhod 73
Ariel 119, 120
Aries 181, 182
Armaros 122
Artemis 73
Ascended Ancestor 149, 150, 151
Ascended Beings 26
Ascended Masters 15, 116, 145, 146,
    147, 149, 150
Ascended masters 148
Asclepius 8, 77, 100, 116, 172, 176
Asgard 66
Ashe 94
Asir 95
Aspecting 109, 110
Aspu 38
Astral 13, 15, 19, 26, 27, 28, 30,
    33, 35, 43, 51, 60, 61, 62,
    63, 67, 70, 71, 72, 73, 75,
    76, 77, 78, 79, 81, 82, 83,
    100, 103, 104, 105, 112, 126,
    127, 129, 130, 146, 151, 166,
    168, 178, 185, 187, 191, 192,
    219, 225, 242
  Library 61, 62, 63
  project 19
Astrology 9, 122, 123, 128, 174,
    175, 180, 181, 243
Astronomers 16, 201
Astrophysics 24, 46
Athena 85, 86, 87
Atoms 42, 43, 44

Atum 46, 47, 172
Audhumla 53
Aura 34, 108, 110, 229
Aurora borealis 201
Azazel 122, 123, 132
Aztecs 87, 206

B

Babylonians 64, 65, 174, 175, 176, 189
Baldar 77
Baraqijal 122
Bestla 53
Bethor 209
Bhakti 98, 99
Bible 22, 70, 121, 126, 171
Bifrost 67
Big Bang 41, 44, 81, 82, 83, 118
Big bang 42
Big Dipper 166
Binah 49, 50, 68, 78, 80, 81, 212, 214, 218
Black Book 131
Black hole 44
Blacksmithing 123
Blavatsky, H.P. 148
Blood 53, 54, 101, 128, 165, 204
Bloodline 149, 150
Book of Enoch 114, 123, 124, 126
Book of the Law 149
Bor 53
Brahma 52, 146, 172
Buddha 17, 77, 146
Buddhism 56, 70, 145, 226, 231, 233, 234
Buri 53

C

Cairo 149
Cancer 168, 176, 181, 183
Canis Major 174, 177
Canis minor 177
Capricorn 184
Cassiopeia 174, 177
Cecrops 85

Celtic 95
Chakras 146, 154, 167
Chalice 118, 120
Chaos 54, 55, 82
Cherokee 32, 166, 176
Chesed 50, 68, 75, 76, 79, 80, 209, 214, 218
Childbirth 198
Chiron 163
Chokmah 49, 69, 70, 79, 80, 81, 82, 214
Christian 9, 14, 22, 44, 93, 114, 115, 122, 128, 132, 134, 135, 139, 170, 177, 226
Chumbley, Andrew 169
Collective consciousness 18
Consciousness 17, 19, 20, 22, 39, 63, 69, 73, 74, 75, 76, 77, 78, 79, 80, 81, 82, 84, 97, 100, 110, 111, 116, 127, 140, 153, 156, 157, 158, 159, 173, 178, 184, 185, 187, 192, 202, 218, 234
Constellation 11, 16, 25, 26, 39, 114, 122, 125, 161, 162, 164, 166, 168, 169, 171, 172, 173, 174, 175, 176, 177, 178, 179, 180, 181, 186, 189, 194
Copper 199
Cosmic 13, 14, 15, 16, 41, 52, 53, 54, 64, 80, 88, 119, 147, 148, 149, 165, 200
  Web 16, 119, 225
Cosmos 11, 24, 29, 31, 40, 52, 63, 78, 87, 170, 173, 230
Coyote 74, 193, 194, 195
Creation 11, 14, 24, 37, 38, 39, 40, 41, 44, 46, 47, 48, 51, 52, 66, 70, 75, 80, 81, 83, 92, 93, 123, 128, 132, 134, 147, 158, 179, 203, 204, 207, 230, 231, 243
Crowley, Aleister 149
Crystal ball 130, 131, 141, 219, 220

Cygnus 177

D

Dead 13, 15, 65, 66, 149, 150, 161, 164, 168, 176, 177, 200, 234, 243

Death 8, 13, 14, 15, 19, 21, 22, 46, 55, 65, 80, 86, 89, 94, 107, 139, 145, 146, 148, 149, 163, 164, 165, 172, 176, 190, 201, 204, 207, 210, 211, 212, 226, 234, 238, 243

Demeter 72

Demonic 20, 115, 121, 123

Demons 14, 17, 108, 115, 118, 119, 123, 128, 129, 176, 209, 220

Destiny 16, 23, 134, 138, 184, 214, 226, 228, 229, 239, 240, 241, 242, 246

Devil 135, 170

Devotions 87, 95, 98, 100, 101, 105, 106, 110, 236, 245

Dharma 226

Diana 22, 73, 106, 108, 164, 175, 177, 190

Dimension 16, 20, 25, 43, 45, 46, 65, 168, 185, 186, 187

Divination 94, 104, 114, 146

Divine Father 49, 82

Divine Mother 49

Divine Will 18, 57, 78, 134, 138, 206, 230, 243

Draco 26, 168, 170, 171, 175, 186

Dragon 136, 170, 175, 206

Dreams 17, 19, 20, 21, 56, 91, 121, 138, 154, 190, 192, 197, 208, 226, 235, 240, 245

Duat 65, 168

E

Ea 38

Eagle 8

Earth 7, 11, 13, 14, 15, 16, 18, 21, 22, 26, 27, 29, 39, 40, 42, 43, 45, 47, 52, 54, 55, 57, 60, 65, 72, 74, 75, 76, 77, 78, 79, 81, 82, 83, 92, 93, 94, 102, 114, 118, 119, 120, 121, 122, 123, 124, 125, 126, 132, 133, 134, 135, 136, 145, 149, 151, 153, 156, 159, 161, 164, 166, 169, 172, 173, 174, 176, 181, 184, 189, 190, 194, 197, 198, 199, 200, 201, 202, 204, 205, 206, 207, 208, 210, 226, 230, 234, 237, 239, 240, 246, 247

Egypt 19, 21, 26, 44, 46, 51, 65, 95, 97, 105, 107, 167, 169, 171, 172, 174, 175, 177, 189, 201, 203, 204, 232, 239

Electromagnetic force 42, 43, 118

Electrons 43

Elements 13, 42, 43, 72, 116, 159, 208, 210, 243

Elves 13, 14, 129, 247

Endymion 190

Enlightened beings 158

Eros 55, 76, 99

Evocation 71, 105, 119, 120, 121, 139, 141

Ezeqeel 122

Ezili Freda 100, 196

F

Faery 13

Fate 16, 55, 92, 239, 241

Fates 243

Father Sky 25, 79

Fears 17, 20, 21, 41, 51, 56, 57, 89, 106, 135, 150, 173

Fifth Dimension 45

Fire 7, 8, 9, 13, 42, 51, 53, 66, 72, 114, 118, 121, 125, 126, 135, 137, 172, 175

Fourth Dimension 45

Frankincense 96, 131, 141, 182

Frau Holda 95

Freya 66, 76

Freyr 66, 76, 95

Frigg 66

G

Gabriel 73, 118, 120

Gaia 72

Galaxy 13, 14, 16, 25, 26, 42, 46, 61, 161, 162, 164, 165, 175, 185, 200

Gamma rays 21, 43, 64, 165

Ganesha 74

Ganges River 90

Geb 47, 65, 72

Geburah 50, 76, 77, 78, 206, 214, 218

Gemini 172, 182, 194

Ginnungagap 53

Giza 168

Gnosis 139, 170, 173, 180, 246

God 8, 11, 15, 39, 47, 48, 50, 54, 55, 70, 74, 76, 82, 83, 86, 89, 93, 94, 97, 98, 99, 101, 102, 103, 106, 111, 114, 116, 118, 121, 123, 124, 125, 126, 128, 132, 133, 134, 135, 136, 139, 145, 158, 164, 167, 168, 172, 205, 214, 215, 230, 237, 242

Goddess 38, 50, 77, 90, 93, 94, 96, 101, 103, 105, 111, 164, 206

Gold 76, 203

Golden Calf 118

Golden Dawn 9, 148

Grandfather Sun 64, 77

Grandmother Moon 64, 73

Gratitude 89, 103, 105, 112, 153, 158, 160

Gravity 42, 44, 45, 118, 165, 191, 207, 208, 210

Great Bear 81

Greco-Roman 7, 8, 54, 67, 97, 135, 163, 171, 175, 176, 177, 190, 205, 210

Greek 21, 23, 44, 67, 87, 95, 107, 114, 116

Greeks 87, 105, 174, 189

Grigori 121, 122, 125, 127

Guardian angel 18

H

Hades 107, 164, 190

Hadit 95

Hagith 199

Haniel 75

Hathor 176

Heal 11, 16, 18, 23, 89, 91, 106, 115, 116, 147, 149, 150, 163, 164, 190, 200, 242, 247

Healer 15, 18, 20, 23, 96, 114, 115, 118, 139, 146, 153, 163, 229, 236, 238, 239, 240, 241, 246

Healing 8, 13, 14, 15, 17, 20, 23, 26, 60, 62, 63, 64, 68, 70, 71, 77, 90, 91, 93, 104, 105, 107, 108, 115, 118, 119, 122, 127, 140, 146, 147, 149, 150, 151, 152, 156, 157, 158, 159, 160, 172, 176, 195, 202, 225, 228, 232, 233, 239, 240, 241

Health 56, 64, 107, 121, 153, 211, 235, 240

Heathen 66, 91, 95, 97

Heavenly spheres 128

Heliopolis 167, 168

Helium 42, 200

Hermes 74, 195

Hero 23, 134, 175, 176
  journey 23

Higher beings 8, 11, 15, 20, 46, 51, 152

Higher Self 16, 17, 21, 31, 77, 157, 160, 202, 203

Hinduism 56, 98, 172, 174, 226, 231, 233

Hippolytus 164

Hod 74, 75, 116, 196, 215, 217
Holy Guardian Angel 18, 77, 202, 203
Holy Medicine People 155, 157, 158
Horus 77, 172
Hydrogen 42, 165, 200, 207, 210

I

Ifa 92, 93, 94, 95, 110
Illusions 20, 138, 192
India 90, 148, 172, 176
Infrared 165
Inipi 202
Inspiration 11, 15, 136, 138, 149
Invocation 105, 106, 108, 109, 137, 170, 219
Iran 131
Iraq 131
Iron 206
Isis 47, 81, 97, 148, 171, 172, 177, 237, 239

J

Jesus 15, 128, 132, 139
Jupiter 60, 61, 79, 171, 184, 202, 206, 207, 208, 210, 215, 218

K

Kabbalistic 9, 15, 18, 44, 48, 67, 68, 93, 98, 119, 127, 145, 212, 217
Kali Ma 81, 90, 209
Karl Von Eckartshausen 147
Karma 92, 99, 145, 181, 195, 209, 211, 225, 226, 227, 229, 234, 239
Keter 49, 50, 68, 70, 76, 80, 82, 84, 93, 126, 127, 214
Key of Solomon 116
Khamael 77
Kheprer 46
Kishar 38
Kokabel 122
Koran 171
Kronos 55, 210

L

Lady Luna 191
Lahmu 38
Lakota 202
Law of Attraction 56, 225
Lead 212
Leo 181, 183
Liberation 145, 234
Libra 183
Lilith 134, 176
Loki 74, 107
Love 9, 21, 22, 47, 50, 55, 56, 67, 75, 86, 88, 89, 94, 98, 99, 100, 103, 104, 107, 122, 132, 150, 185, 190, 196, 197, 198, 202, 205, 207, 209, 221, 226, 228, 231, 234, 241, 245
Lucifer 99, 134, 135, 136, 137, 138, 141, 170, 197, 230
Lugh 78
Lwa 100

M

Maat 65
Magick mirror 130, 140, 141, 219, 220
Malchuth 50, 68, 71, 72, 73, 75, 76, 77, 78, 79, 81, 82, 83, 118, 215, 216
Manni 73
Marduk 38, 39, 175
Mars 60, 77, 78, 159, 171, 182, 203, 204, 205, 210, 215, 217
Masters 148
Mathers, S.L. MacGregor 116, 148
Maya 44
Medicine 15, 20, 34, 56, 121, 154, 155, 159, 202, 239
    Elders 156
    wheel 156
Meditation 52, 57, 58, 68, 95, 101, 102, 110, 157, 179
Mediterranean Sea 167
Medusa 176

Melek Taus 131, 132, 141

Mercury 60, 74, 118, 171, 182, 183, 193, 194, 195, 196, 211, 215, 217

Mescalero Apache 152

Mesopotamia 38, 87

Metatron 82, 118, 126, 127

Michael 48, 74, 118, 120, 158, 170

Middleworld 12, 13, 29, 36

Midwinter 201

Midworld 14, 17, 20, 34, 60, 66, 104, 247

Milky Way 26, 42, 61, 64, 167, 200

Moon 11, 13, 22, 39, 42, 57, 65, 68, 73, 106, 108, 114, 119, 122, 125, 164, 172, 183, 189, 190, 191, 192, 203, 215, 217
 Full 191

Mother 50, 55, 72, 80, 93, 97, 237
 Earth 55, 72, 97

Multiverse 24, 26, 44, 45, 83

Music 23, 118

Muslims 132

Muspellheim 53, 66

N

Natal chart 161, 181

Native American 15, 19, 24, 64, 89, 93, 95, 107, 108, 116, 151, 152, 154, 155, 160, 166, 176, 195

Nature spirits 13, 60, 191, 247

Nebulas 165

Nemesis 55

Nephilim 122, 123, 124, 128, 141

Nephthys 47, 172

Netzach 75, 76, 116, 199, 215, 217

Neutrinos 43

Niflheim 53, 66, 121, 124

Nile 26, 167, 171, 177

Nirvana 146, 198

Njord 66

Noah 124

Nordic 12, 21, 44, 51, 52, 66, 87, 107, 175

Norns 243

Nuit/Nut 65, 95

Nun 46

Nymphs 174

O

Och 203

Odin 53, 66, 79, 95, 107, 239

Offerings 86, 87, 89, 90, 91, 95, 98, 100, 103, 105, 112, 130, 137, 140, 174, 202, 242

Old Testament 114

Olodumare 92, 93

Olorun 92, 93

Olympus 67, 86, 189

Ophiel 196

Ophiuchus 164, 172, 176

Ori 94

Orion 162, 166, 168, 172, 174, 175, 177, 178, 179

Orishas 93

Osiris 47, 105, 167, 168, 172, 175, 237, 239

Otherworld 13, 25, 61, 65, 149

OTO 95

P

Pan 25, 72

Pangu 53, 54

Parallel universe 46

Past life 232, 233, 234

Peacock Angel 131, 132

Pentacle 119, 120

Pentagram 115

Perseus 176

Phalegh 206

Pharaoh 105

Phul 192

Pisces 181, 185

Planet 8, 9, 11, 13, 14, 34, 39, 42, 53, 54, 57, 61, 65, 70, 114, 118, 119, 156, 161, 162, 166, 171, 181, 182, 189, 192, 194, 195, 197, 198, 200, 204,

205, 207, 208, 210, 211, 212, 215, 217, 218, 220, 221, 222, 225

Planetary spirits 20, 21, 129, 140, 219, 221

Pleiades 166, 172, 174, 176

Pluto 107, 184

Poetry 15, 189

Poseidon 79, 85, 86

Possession 110

Primordial Egg 83

Prometheus 7, 8, 135

Protostar 165

Psyche 99

Psychology 17, 20

Pyramids 19, 65, 168, 169, 201

Q

Quan Yin 76

Quantum-physics 40

Quarks 43

Quasars 42

Quetzalcoatl 144, 206

R

Ra 25, 46, 82, 95, 167, 172, 175, 203, 204

Radio waves 21, 43, 207

Raphael 76, 115, 118, 119, 140, 158

Ratziel 81

Rebirth 13, 65, 145, 185, 209

Reiki 116, 146, 147, 152, 160, 236, 238, 241

Masters 146

Reincarnation 95, 145, 161, 231, 234

Retribution 55

Rhea 81

Rigel 169

Rome 107, 210

S

Sabbatic Craft 169

Sacrifice 7, 9, 88, 89, 100, 103, 144, 184, 200, 205, 206

Human 144

Sage 68, 96, 131, 182

Sagittarius 184

Saints 146

Sandalphon 72

Sandalwood 96, 182

Sangreal 127

Sariel 122

Satan 118, 128, 132, 135, 170

Saturn 60, 80, 81, 171, 184, 209, 210, 211, 215, 218, 221, 222

Saturnalia 210

Scorpio 184

Scrying 63, 130, 131, 140, 141, 219, 220, 221

Seckmeth 78

Secret Chiefs 148

Secret Doctrine 148

Sekhmet 203, 204

Semjaza 122

Sephiroth 44, 49, 50, 67, 68, 70, 72, 73, 75, 79, 116, 130, 141, 214, 215, 216, 217, 218, 221

Septagram
Ritual 212

Seth 47

Shadow self 17, 21

Shakti 81

Shamsiel 122

Shinto 44

Shiva 82, 96, 209

Shu 47

Silver 192

Sirius 168, 169, 171, 172, 177

Sleep 55, 91, 160, 190

Smithcraft 206

Sol 192, 199

Solar system 60, 191, 197, 200, 204, 207, 208

Solar Wind 201

Soul 9, 31, 32, 56, 65, 94, 135, 145, 164, 181, 185, 197, 230, 232

Source of All things 49, 83, 86

Space 11, 15, 16, 20, 25, 29, 31, 35, 38, 40, 42, 47, 49, 51, 60, 61, 64, 71, 72, 89, 100, 102, 104, 105, 107, 115, 119, 122, 123, 124, 129, 140, 141, 142, 156, 165, 173, 178, 179, 187, 190, 205, 212, 218, 219, 220, 221, 222, 230
Spiritual evolution 15, 24, 48, 116, 126, 128, 146, 149, 173, 179, 181, 225, 229, 231, 240
Spiritual purpose 18, 149, 230
St. Germain 146
Staff 19, 119
Star Nation 161, 166
Stars 8, 9, 11, 14, 16, 19, 25, 34, 39, 42, 52, 53, 54, 57, 64, 65, 87, 114, 122, 125, 126, 128, 136, 160, 161, 164, 165, 166, 167, 168, 169, 170, 171, 172, 173, 174, 176, 177, 178, 179, 180, 181, 185, 186, 187, 189, 197, 199, 200, 201, 207
  portals 16, 25, 122, 181, 186
Stonehenge 201
Strife 55
Strong nuclear force 42, 43, 118
Subatomic particles 64, 165
Sumbel 91
Sun 7, 8, 11, 22, 23, 39, 42, 57, 60, 61, 65, 76, 87, 114, 118, 122, 125, 127, 144, 153, 159, 165, 171, 172, 174, 183, 193, 194, 197, 199, 200, 201, 202, 203, 204, 207, 208, 210, 211, 215, 217, 221, 222, 238
Sundance 202
Sunna 77
Sunrise Ceremony 153
Sunset Ceremony 153
Surt 66
Sweat lodge 202
Sword 118, 120
Symbols 21, 24, 63, 121, 161, 171, 189, 191
Syria 131

T

Takata, Grand Master 147
Talismans 71, 98, 116
Tartarus 55
Taurus 169, 182
Technology 7, 8, 43, 121, 123, 135, 196
Tefnut 47
Temple 8, 71, 90, 96, 100, 102, 104, 107, 119, 124, 139, 140, 144, 167, 168, 179, 202, 212, 217
Thelema 149
Theosophical Society 148
Theseus 164
Thor 25, 66, 79, 95
Thoth 74, 172
Three Worlds 12, 20, 31, 102
Thunder Beings 15, 24, 64, 151
Tiamat 38, 39
Tibet 148
Tibetan Book of the Dead 234
Time 7, 15, 20, 24, 32, 33, 34, 36, 38, 40, 43, 45, 48, 49, 51, 57, 60, 61, 62, 67, 88, 89, 96, 98, 99, 100, 101, 103, 104, 108, 109, 110, 114, 115, 120, 124, 131, 136, 137, 139, 147, 148, 150, 151, 152, 154, 155, 156, 157, 160, 161, 166, 170, 176, 179, 190, 191, 195, 197, 200, 201, 205, 210, 216, 219, 222, 225, 228, 231, 233, 235, 236, 237, 240, 241, 243, 244
Tin 208
Tiphereth 50, 76, 77, 78, 79, 81, 82, 84, 116, 127, 203, 215, 217
Tobacco 194
Toltec 144

Tonka Shaila 82
Torch 7
Totem 25, 29, 31, 32, 33, 34, 35, 36, 151
Traditional Witchcraft 48, 49, 95, 97, 114, 121, 122, 123, 127, 135, 169, 170, 175, 229
Treasures 8
Tree of Life 48, 49, 67, 68, 70, 72, 98, 127, 130, 212, 217, 218
Triangle of Art 219
Trilithons 201
Tubal Cain 95, 122, 123, 170
Tyr 78
Tzadkiel 79
Tzaphkiel 80

U
Ultraviolet 165
Underworld 12, 13, 14, 17, 19, 20, 21, 34, 50, 60, 65, 104, 107, 149, 150, 164, 168, 173, 199, 232, 244
Upperworld Dragon 175
Uranus 82, 185
Uriel 119, 159
Ursa Major 166, 168, 172, 175
Ursa Minor 167, 168
Usui, Grand Master Dr. 146

V
Valhalla 66
Ve 53
Vedas 52, 181
Venus 60, 75, 76, 97, 136, 171, 182, 184, 196, 197, 198, 205, 215, 217
Vile 53
Virgo 183

Vishnu 52
Vodou 95, 100, 101, 110, 196
Void 46, 53, 70

W
Watchers 121, 122, 124, 128, 141
Water 13, 30, 31, 38, 42, 43, 46, 72, 83, 87, 90, 93, 102, 103, 104, 118, 177, 191, 210, 219, 237
Waylands Smithy 169
Weak nuclear force 42, 43, 118
Witchblood 127
Wonka Tonka 83, 202
World Tree 12, 13, 24, 25, 29, 30, 31, 33, 35, 60, 66, 151
Wyrd 92

X
X-rays 43, 165

Y
Yama 172
Yesod 50, 73, 74, 75, 76, 77, 78, 79, 81, 82, 83, 116, 127, 192, 215, 217
Yezidi 131, 132, 133, 134
Yggdrasil 12, 44, 66, 200
Ymir 53
Yoruba 94

Z
Zeus 7, 25, 79, 164, 174, 175, 210, 243
Zodiac 26, 81, 125, 168, 171, 180, 181, 182, 186